Marx's Economics

P.N. JUNANKAR
University of Essex

HERITAGE

Heritage Publishers
NEW DELHI 1989

First published in India by
HERITAGE PUBLISHERS
4-C, Ansari Road, New Delhi
In arrangement with
PHILIP ALLAN PUBLISHERS LIMITED
OXFORD OX5 4SE

Reissued 1989

British Library Cataloguing in Publication Data

Junankar, P.N.
Marx's economics.
1. Marxian economics
I. Title
335.4 HB97.5
ISBN 0-86003-026-1
ISBN 0-86003-125-X Pbk

Set in 10/11 pt Paladium by MHL Typesetting Limited, Coventry
Printed in Great Britain at The Camelot Press Limited, Southampton

Contents

Preface

This book is based on a ten-week course of lectures I have been giving at the University of Essex since 1973. I have benefited enormously from comments and criticisms from several generations of students. I am grateful for encouragement and comments from Professors A.B. Atkinson, A. Asimakopulos, W.J. Baumol, M. Blaug, D. McLellan, Dr. G. Catephores and Dr. Paul Sweezy. They are not, of course, responsible for any remaining errors, or for my prejudices. I should like to thank my father for having instilled in me an interest in Marx's writings and for helpful comments from a philosophical viewpoint. I should also like to thank my wife for her patience and encouragement during the long gestation period of this book. Finally, I should like to thank Sheila Ogden for doing an excellent job in converting my illegible scrawl into an excellent typescript.

To My Father

Acknowledgements

I am grateful to the following for permission to reprint from previously published material:

1. Lawrence & Wishart Ltd, London

   Maurice Cornforth (1977) *Materialism & the Dialectical Method.*
   Karl Marx (1977) *Capital* Volumes I, II and III.
   Karl Marx & Friedrich Engels (1962) *Selected Works* Volumes I and II.
   Karl Marx & Friedrich Engvls (1975—) *Collected Works* Volumes 1— .

2. Penguin Books, Harmondsworth

   Karl Marx (1973) *Grundrisse*, translated by Martin Nicolaus (Pelican Marx Library/New Left Review, 1973) pp. 99—100, 221. Translation and Foreword copyright © Martin Nicolaus, 1973. Reprinted by permission of Penguin Books Ltd.

3. Random House, New York

   Karl Marx (1973) *Grundrisse: Foundations of the Critique of Political Economy.* Translated with a Foreword by Martin Nicolaus. Copyright © Random House Inc 1973 for USA and Canada.

4. Progress Publishers, Moscow

   Karl Marx *Theories of Surplus Value* (Volume IV of *Capital*).
   Part I (1963, 1969).
   Part II (1968).
   Part III (1971).
   Karl Marx (1970) *A Contribution to the Critique of Political Economy.*
   Karl Marx & Friedrich Engels (1975) *Selected Correspondence*, 3rd edition.

5. Professor Anwar Shaikh, Department of Economics, The Graduate Faculty, New School for Social Research, New York.
   Tables 3.2 and 3.3 (pp. 53 and 57) are reproduced from his article, 'Marx's theory of value and the "transformation problem"' (1977).

List of Abbreviations

Works by Marx and Engels

(For details of publisher etc., see Bibliography at the end of the book)

CW Vol . . .	Collected Works Volume . . .
Critique	*Contribution to a Critique of Political Economy*
KI, KII, KIII	*Capital* Volumes I, II and III respectively
SC	*Selected Correspondence*
SWI, SWII	*Selected Works* Volumes I and II
TSVI, TSVII, TSVIII	*Theories of Surplus Value* Parts I, II and III respectively

Notation

$\hat{C}$	Commodities
$\hat{C}(C)$	Commodities in the Commodity Domain
$\hat{C}(DP)$	Commodities valued at Direct Prices
$\hat{C}(P)$	Commodities in the Price Domain (at Prices of Production)
$\hat{C}(V)$	Commodities in the Value Domain
L or LP	Labour Power
M	Money
P	Prices of Production
$\hat{P}$ or PC	Productive Capital
s	surplus value
s'	rate of surplus value or rate of exploitation
π	rate of profit
c	constant capital
v	variable capital
w	total value of output of a Department or the per unit value of a commodity.

Mathematical Notation

$>$	greater than
$<$	less than
$=$	equal to
$\neq$	not equal to
$f'(\ )$	first derivative of a function $f(\ )$. It gives the slope of the curve; $f'(\ ) < 0$ means a downward sloping curve from left to right and $f'(\ ) > 0$ an upward sloping curve.

The philosphers have only interpreted the world in various ways; the point however is to change it.

(Theses on Feuerbach)

1 Introduction

1.1 Aims/Objectives

The aim of this book is to provide an introduction to Marx's economics: specifically to explain the underlying model in Marx's voluminous writings. The book is based mainly on the mature Marx: on *Capital* and *Theories of Surplus Value*. References to earlier work will be made mainly to supplement this interpretation, rather than to provide an account of the development of Marx's economic thought.[1] Although it would be valuable to do so, I shall *not* be comparing Marx with Classical writers (e.g. Smith, the Physiocrats, Ricardo), nor with neo-Classical writers (e.g. Arrow, Hahn, Samuelson). The focus of interest will be the theoretical and analytical structure of Marx's *economics*. Although I shall refer to social, political, philosophical and historical factors, they will be treated only in so far as they are *directly* relevant to explaining Marx's economics. Having thus limited the scope of this book, I hope that I shall be able to highlight the important features of Marx's economics. In my view, the key to understanding Marx is to view the economic system as a system in *motion* with opposing forces (the 'dialectic') interacting. In Marx's view, the two major forces in a capitalist economy are, of course, the bourgeoisie and the proletariat and he saw as fundamental to the relation between capital and labour the concept of exploitation. In a capitalist system the exploitation of labour is 'veiled' by market forces. It is Marx's intention to remove the 'cloak' of market relations which veils the underlying reality of exploitation and degradation of the working class.

1.2 Background Information on Marx[2]

(a) Life

Karl Marx was born in Trier in Germany in 1818. He studied law at the University of Bonn and then at the University of Berlin. In Berlin he came into contact with Hegelian philosophy and he joined a radical group called the 'Young Hegelians'. In 1843 he married Jenny von Westphalen and emigrated to Paris. Soon after, he met Friedrich Engels and their friendship was a lifelong one and the collaboration in their work so close that it is difficult to distinguish their separate contributions.[3] (When I refer to Marx's economics, or Marxian economics, I am using it as a short-hand to refer to Marx and Engels' economics.) After a brief spell in Germany which ended in expulsion, in 1849 he finally moved to London where he spent the rest of his life. Engels also moved to England to join his father's business, the profits of which helped to subsidise the impoverished Marx family in London. Marx died in London on 13 March 1883 and was buried in Highgate Cemetery.

(b) Works on Economics[4]

Marx was greatly impressed by reading Engels' *Outlines of a Critique of Political Economy* (1843) which was published in the *Deutsch-Französische Jahrbücher* in 1844 (*CW* Vol. 3). It may have been the catalyst that turned Marx's attention to economic studies. His early writings on economics include *Economic and Philosophic Manuscripts* (1844) which was published posthumously (*CW* Vol. 3); *Poverty of Philosophy* (1847) (*CW* Vol. 6); *The Communist Manifesto* (1848) (with Engels, *CW* Vol. 6); *The Grundrisse* (preparatory manuscripts for *Capital* written in 1857—58 and first published in English (in complete form) in 1973; and *A Contribution to the Critique of Political Economy* (1859) which was received by the world with a deafening silence! The first volume of *Capital* was published in 1867 (*KI*). The second and third volumes were edited by Engels after Marx's death from manuscripts at varying stages of completion. Volume II (*KII*) appeared in 1885 and Volume III (*KIII*) in 1894. *Theories of Surplus Value*, written in 1861—63, which was to be the fourth volume of *Capital*, was not published until much later when it was edited by Karl Kautsky and published in three parts between 1905 and 1910. *Wages, Price and Profit*, a lecture given by Marx to the International Working Men's Association in 1865 and first published in 1898 (*SWI*), provides a good introduction to Marx's economics.

It is important to remember that Marx's writings were aimed at different audiences and were therefore emphasising different aspects of the subject and /or simplifying various aspects. Some of them were obviously propagandist (the *Manifesto*) and some obviously polemical (*Poverty of Philosophy*). However, a major problem in assessing Marx's work is that only the first volume of his *magnum opus, Capital*, was published during his lifetime. Volumes 2 and 3 had to be put together and deciphered from various manuscripts and fragments in his well-known illegible scrawl. Fortunately for us, Engels had collaborated with Marx to such an extent that an almost coherent whole has been published. Most people, both friends and foes of Marx, have read only the *Manifesto* and perhaps *Wages, Price and Profit*, which were propagandist in nature; but to appreciate his work there is no alternative to struggling through (at least) *Capital!*

(c) Debts and Credits

Marx belonged to a now dying tradition of social scientists who encompassed politics, sociology, economics, history and philosophy. Schumpeter has, very correctly, called him 'the greatest social scientist'.[5] Marx began his academic career in law and philosophy and eventually became an economist. He began his working career as a journalist writing brilliant pieces for the *Rheinische Zeitung* and later for the *New York Tribune*. His political views led to him being hounded from Germany, Belgium and France, until he found a safe haven in England. He was, of course, a revolutionary and was active in forming the First International (1864). His political activities prevented him from completing his economic writings. He had a tremendous appetite for reading: he read books in several languages — French, German (of course), English, Latin, Greek, Italian and Russian. Late in life he even began learning calculus.

His intellectual debts are numerous, but probably most importantly to Hegel (Philosophy), to the French socialists (Fourier,

Proudhon) and to the English Classical economists (Adam Smith, David Ricardo) and the French Physiocrats (Quesnay, Turgot). Lenin has said that to really understand Marx you must read Hegel[6], but then you may never finish reading (or understanding) Hegel! It seems to me that some knowledge of Hegel may be adequate before beginning on the mammoth task of reading *Capital.* On the economics side, to really understand Marx you have to read Adam Smith's *Wealth of Nations* and David Ricardo's *Principles of Political Economy.*

To mention Marx's intellectual debts is in no way to under-rate his contributions. He was obviously a product of his environment: Marx's economics was an intellectual response to previous economic writings, but also an intellectual response to the development of capitalism in Europe, especially Britain. In some ways he was a Classical economist, but in fact he provided an entirely new paradigm.[7]

1.3 Methods of Analysis

(a) Philosophical

As mentioned earlier, Marx was influenced by Hegel. From Hegel he learned the *dialectical method.* The Hegelian influence on Marx is especially noticeable in his earlier writings e.g. *Grundrisse,* but less so in *Capital.* It has been argued by some writers that Marx's analysis for *Capital* is Hegelian, but the form of presentation has been 'purified' of Hegelian language to make it easier to digest. The dialectical method consists in studying a process in motion and change which results from contradictory aspects of a phenomenon. Everything is conceived of as being in motion/changing: nature, methods of production, society, the intellectual world.[8] Each phenomenon consists of contradictory elements (the so-called 'internal contradictions') which contain the seeds of its destruction. A good summary is provided below:

> Dialectical materialism considers the universe, not as static, not as unchanging, but as in continual process of development. It considers this development, not as a smooth, continuous and unbroken process, but as a process in which phases of gradual evolutionary change are interrupted by breaks in continuity, by the sudden leap from one state to another. And it seeks for the explanation, the driving force, of this universal movement, not in inventions of idealist fantasy, but within material processes themselves — in the inner contradictions, the opposite conflicting tendencies, which are in operation in every process of nature and society.
> (Cornforth 1977a, p. 53)

The materialist conception of history is that all intellectual, social, political processes/movements are determined by the mode of production. Each stage in history has antagonistic elements and contains the seeds of its own destruction. Each stage survives only until it has reached maturity and allowed the productive forces to be fully developed. When the social/institutional framework no longer allows the productive forces to develop, there is a social change, which may be revolutionary. This dialectical process is sometimes conceived of as a sequence of 'thesis-antithesis-synthesis.'[9] A feature of dialectics is that quantitative change leads to qualitative change. A common example is that when you apply heat to water gradually, the water first gets hot and then after a certain critical point turns into steam. Social phenomena are viewed similarly, e.g. increasing numbers in the working class eventually leads to a change in society.

A classic statement of these ideas is given by Marx in the *Preface to the Critique of Political Economy* which is quoted below:

> In the social production of their life, men enter into definite relations that are indispensable and independent of their will, relations of production which correspond to a definite state of development of their material productive forces. The sum total of these relations of production constitutes the economic structure of society, the real foundation, on which rises a legal and political superstructure and to which correspond definite forms of social consciousness. The mode of production of material life conditions the social, political and intellectual life process in general. It is not the consciousness of men that determines their being, but, on the contrary, their social being that determines their consciousness. At a certain stage of their development, the material productive forces of society come in conflict with the existing relations of production, or — what is but a legal expression for the same thing — with the property relations within which they have been at work hitherto. From forms of development of the productive forces these relations turn into their fetters. Then begins an epoch of social revolution. With the change of the economic foundation the entire immense superstructure is more or less rapidly transformed. In considering such transformations a distinction should always be made between the material transformation of the economic conditions of production, which can be determined with the precision of natural science, and the legal, political, religious, aesthetic or philosophic — in short, ideological forms in which men become conscious of this conflict and fight it out. Just as our opinion of an individual is not based on what he thinks of himself, so can we not judge of such a period of transformation by its own consciousness; on the contrary, this consciousness must be explained rather from the contradictions of material life, from the existing conflict between the social productive forces and the relations of production. No social order ever perishes before all the productive forces for which there is room in it have

> developed; and new, higher relations of production never appear before the material conditions of their existence have matured in the womb of the old society itself. Therefore mankind always sets itself only such tasks as it can solve; since, looking at the matter more closely, it will always be found that the task itself arises only when the material conditions for its solution already exist or are at least in the process of formation. In broad outlines Asiatic, ancient, feudal and modern bourgeois modes of production can be designated as progressive epochs in the economic formation of society. The bourgeois relations of production are the last antagonistic form of the social process of production — antagonistic not in the sense of individual antagonism, but of one arising from the social conditions of life of the individuals; at the same time the productive forces developing in the womb of bourgeois society create the material conditions for the solution of that antagonism. This social formation brings, therefore, the prehistory of human society to a close.
>
> (*SWI*, pp. 362—4)

The best account of historical materialism is to be found in Marx and Engels' *German Ideology* (On Feuerbach) (*CW* Vol. 5), although the best known account is in the Manifesto when they assert defiantly, 'the history of all hitherto existing society is the history of class struggles.' (*SWI*, p. 34)

The view that history can be divided up into stages or epochs is scattered in Marx and Engels' writings. For example, in *Poverty of Philosophy* Marx argues:

> Social relations are closely bound up with productive forces. In acquiring new productive forces men change their mode of production; and in changing their mode of production, in changing the way of earning their living, they change all their social relations. The hand-mill gives you society with the feudal lord; the steam-mill society with the industrial capitalist.
>
> (*CW* Vol. 6, p. 166)

Similarly, Engels argues:

> . . . the final cause of all social changes and political revolutions are to be sought, not in men's brains, . . ., but in changes in the modes of production and exchange. They are to be sought not in the philosophy, but in the economics of each particular epoch.
>
> (*Socialism: Utopian and Scientific*, *SW* II, p. 136.)

The development of society is viewed as a progression of different stages (or epochs) of history which correspond to different forms of property ownership. 'The various stages of development in the division of labour are just so many different forms of property, i.e., the existing stage in the division of labour determines also the relations of individuals to one another with reference to the material, instrument and product of labour.' (Marx and Engels, *German Ideology, CW*, Vol. 5, p. 32). These different stages[10] can be summarised as:

1. Tribal ownership
2. Ancient communal ownership
3. Feudal
4. Capitalist
5. Socialist/Communist.

In each stage, but the last, the forces of production come into conflict with the relations of production and a social change takes place.

In a capitalist society the antagonistic forces, the capitalists and the proletariat, form a unified whole in production, but are in conflict in the distribution of national income. For example, this contradiction of capitalism, the socialised nature of production and the individual nature of property, expresses itself in an 'antagonism of the proletariat and bourgeoisie' (Engels, *Socialism: Utopian and Scientific, SW* II, p. 141).

To summarise, Marx conceives of history as a dialectical movement and emphasises the over-riding importance of the mode of production. He emphasises the class nature of society and the resolution of conflicts by the development of a new form of society.

(b) Economics

As a social scientist, Marx believed in the use of abstraction to analyse economic problems so as to isolate certain key variables. He would begin at a very high level of abstraction and then move step by step towards the more concrete.[11] The purpose of a science, for him, was to remove the veil of appearances from phenomena in order to analyse the underlying reality or essence. It is possible to view *Capital* as the unfolding of this method of analysis. Volume 1 of *Capital* (Capitalist Production) is at a high level of abstraction and the analysis is in the 'value domain' (see below p. 00). Volume 2 (*The Process of Circulation of Capital*) discusses less abstract matters, viz., circulation (or exchange as we would now call it). Volume 3 (*Capitalist Production as a Whole*) descends to a more concrete level by analysing economic phenomena in the 'price domain', studying production, exchange and distribution as a unified whole. Although Volume 1 is primarily about 'production', it is predicated on the basis of exchange (circulation). Similarly, although Volume 2 is about circulation, it is predicated on the basis of production. Volume 3 attempts to provide an integrated analysis of a capitalist economy. Remembering our earlier discussion on historical materialism, it is not surprising that *Capital* begins with production. The dialectical nature of *Capital* is presaged in the following extract from the *Grundrisse:*

> The conclusion we reach is not that production, distribution, exchange and consumption are identical, but that they all form the members of a totality, distinctions within a unity. Production predominates not only over itself, in the antithetical definition of production, but over the other moments as well. The process always returns to production to begin anew. That exchange and consumption cannot be predominant is self-evident. Likewise, distribution as distribution of products; while as distribution of the agents of production it is itself a moment of production. A definite production thus determines a definite consumption distribution and exchange as well as *definite relations between these different moments.* Admittedly, however, *in its one-sided form,* production is itself determined by the other moments. For example, if the market, i.e. the sphere of exchange, expands, then production grows in quantity and the divisions between its different branches become deeper. A change in distribution changes production e.g. concentration of capital, different distribution of the population between town and country, etc. Finally, the needs of consumption determine production. Mutual interaction takes place between the different moments. This is the case with every organic whole.
>
> (pp. 99—100)

It is also important to remember that Marx argued that man was distinguished from animals not by his *thinking* capacity, but by the fact that man *produces* (see *Contribution to a Critique of Political Economy) Theories of Surplus Value* (which was to be Volume 4) shows Marx's skills at analysing, evaluating and debating with earlier writers. The numerous references to the literature suggest an almost encyclopaedic reading and understanding of the extant works on economics.

His economic thinking was in many ways very classical, influenced by Adam Smith, the Physiocrats and Ricardo. Although he criticised them, he gave them credit for having what Schumpeter calls 'vision'. One main distinguishing feature was that while the Classical school was attempting to discover *universal* economic laws (laws that are unchanging over time or social system), Marx argued that economic laws were *historically specific.* Changes in the modes of production would lead to *different* economic laws. Thus the economic laws that determined feudal behaviour would *not* be relevant in a capitalist economy. He would argue that there are some natural laws, but their operation is *modified* under different modes of production.

1.4 Economic Analysis: An Overview

Very briefly the underlying features of Marx's *economic* model are:

(i) *The Importance of Production* (see above)

(ii) *Competition* In most of Marx's analysis he assumes a developed capitalist economy with no restrictions on trade or movements of capital and labour. In effect, he assumes a competitive framework with many buyers and many sellers in all markets. Profit maximisation by capitalists leads to movement of capital to sectors with the highest rates of profits, which *tends* to lead to an equalisation of profit *rates* and bring market prices towards their long-run equilibrium levels ('natural prices'). Unlike the rarefied atmosphere of modern competitive models, he does not assume perfect information. More importantly, for Marx the competitive process contains the seeds of its own destruction: there are inherent forces that lead the system to its antithesis — monopoly. (Remember dialectical materialism.)

(iii) *General Equilibrium* or at least the *inter-relatedness* of the different sectors of the economy. This important 'vision' that Smith and the Physiocrats had plays an important role in Marx's system. Again, this concept of general equilibrium is different from the Walrasian concepts which bourgeois (orthodox) economists learn/teach. Marx's general equilibrium is closer to that of von Neumann. (See Morishima (1973).)

(iv) *Macro-Economic System* Marx was primarily concerned with what we would today call Macroeconomics. In a sense he was a precursor of Keynes in emphasising the importance of accumulation (investment), employment and unemployment etc.

(v) *Income Distribution* Like Ricardo, he believed that income distribution was of primary importance in economics, but unlike him the laws that governed income distribution between the classes were *historical.*

(vi) *Levels of Analysis* Marx's analysis can be viewed on three levels or domains: (a) commodity domain (b) value domain and (c) price domain. Commodities are heterogeneous and we can view economic relations in terms of commodities (but this is to be subject to what he calls 'commodity fetishism', see Chapter 2). Because commodities are heterogeneous, aggregation is difficult. Analysis in the value domain (see Chapter 2) is at a high level of abstraction. Values (in terms of socially necessary labour) can be used for aggregation. The price domain is the one which considers market relations. This is at a more concrete level. However, analysis at this level is 'superficial'.

1.5 Central Concepts: An Overview

(i) *Class*

Unlike the Classical school (e.g. Smith) who believed in the *harmony* of classes, Marx emphasised the importance of class and class *conflict.* Class was defined in an objective way with respect to the means of production. In a capitalist economy he considered the two major classes were the capitalists (bourgeoisie) and the workers (proletariat): those who owned the means of production and those who did not.[12]

(ii) *Labour Theory of Value*

Marx employs the labour theory of value to analyse economic relations. Value is determined by the amount of socially necessary labour embodied. Unlike Ricardo, Marx applies the labour theory of value to *labour itself* i.e. the value of labour *power* (services) is determined by the socially necessary labour embodied. Exploitation was a *necessary* consequence of capitalism; it was a normal process resulting from the nature of capitalist production and exchange. Labour was exploited, not because of accidental cheating or individual 'nasty' capitalists. Labour was not exploited due to monopolistic elements in the economy. Labour was exploited in a *competitive* economy because the worker is paid the value of his *labour power* and the employer gets the *use value* of this labour power. By labour power Marx means 'the aggregate of those mental and physical capabilities existing in a human being, which he exercises whenever he produces a use value of any description.' (*KI*, Ch. 6, p. 167). It is this exploitation of 'surplus value' which provides a *pure surplus* which is the basis of capitalist profits. Marx, like Classical economists before him, was concerned to show the origin and nature of profits which resulted from *production*, not circulation (exchange). (The Physiocrats believed that the only pure surplus came from land (the *produit net*), and Ricardo believed that 'rent' was a pure surplus.) For Marx, circulation could not explain the origin of profits, but simply its distribution: if profits derived for *one* capitalist from exchange, this would net out in aggregate and the nature of profits would be unexplained. (See Chapter 2.)

(iii) *Capital Accumulation*

This plays a central role in Marx's analysis. Capital accumulation brings together with it technological change. With capital accumulation goes increasing concentration of capital: increasing monopolisation and centralisation (take-overs).

> The restless never ending process of profit making alone is what he [the capitalist] aims at. This boundless greed after riches, this passionate chase after exchange values, is common to the capitalist and miser; but while the miser is merely a capitalist gone mad, the capitalist is a rational miser.
>
> (*KI*, Ch. 4, pp. 152—3, square brackets added.) (See Chapter 4)

(iv) *Falling Rate of Profit*

Increasing capital accumulation leads to an increasing organic composition of capital (the ratio of constant to variable capital, or very loosely the capital/labour ratio) which leads to a fall in the rate of profit. The notion of a falling rate of profit has a very long and distinguished pedigree (e.g. Smith, Ricardo), however for Marx this comes about *because* of capital accumulation, rather than due to the 'niggardliness of nature'. For Marx, the causes of the falling rate of profit are to be found in the sphere of production, not circulation (exchange). (See Chapter 5.)

(v) *Industrial Reserve Army*

Capital accumulation is labour saving and makes labour redundant. This pool of unemployed workers puts a downward pressure on wages. Technological unemployment was a relatively unorthodox view among the Classical economists: Malthus was an outlier, and even Ricardo only brought in his famous chapter 'On Machinery' at a late stage. The concept of a secularly increasing industrial reserve army at that juncture of the development of capitalism was, and even now remains, a controversial aspect of economics. (See Chapter 6.)

(vi) *Expanded Reproduction*

Marx provided an interesting analysis of money and circulation which, in effect, was the first growth model of the von Neumann or Harrod type. In this he was far ahead of his time and unfortunately this aspect of his economics was neglected for a long time, except by Feldman in the 1920s in the USSR and later by von Neumann and Harrod. (See Chapters 7 and 8.)

(vii) *Crises*

Crises or the industrial trade cycle, for Marx, was a necessary consequence of capitalist production. The 'relations of production' come into conflict with the 'forces of production' due to the anarchic (plan-less) nature of capitalism. Increasing capital accumulation leads to a falling rate of profit, which after a critical point, leads to a cut back in accumulation and hence a crisis. Increasing capital accumulation leads to increasing productive capacity, but also to increasing unemployment, so that there is underconsumption (realisation crises). Marx argued that these crises were the way in which the internal contradictions of capitalism were resolved, and these crises would recur with increasing severity. Again, except for Sismondi and Malthus, most Classical economists were, in effect, adherents of Say who believed that 'supply creates its own demand'. (See Chapter 9.)

(vii) *Political Economy*

As mentioned in the previous section, Marx's analysis stresses the *unity* of social science. Although I shall be looking at Marx's *economics*, it must be put in its proper *social/political/historical* context. It is impossible to study economics in isolation.

1.6 Marx on Communist Society

Marx had a passionate concern for humanity and the freedom of the individual. However, unlike bourgeois (liberal) concerns about *political* freedom, he believed that true freedom could not exist until the individual had economic freedom. And economic freedom could not come until the society's productive forces had been fully developed under capitalism. The bourgeoisie has 'accomplished wonders far surpassing Egyptian pyramids, Roman aqueducts, and Gothic cathedrals . . .' (*The Communist Manifesto, CW* Vol. 6, p. 487). That freedom (for Marx) depends on having achieved economic freedom is best illustrated from the following passage in the *German Ideology:*

> It is possible to achieve real liberation only in the real world and by real means, that slavery cannot be abolished without the steam-engine and the mule jenny, serfdom cannot be abolished without improved agriculture, and that, in general, people cannot be liberated as long as they are unable to obtain food and drink, housing and clothing in adequate quality and quantity.
>
> (*CW*, Vol. 5, p. 38)

At times Marx's criticisms of capitalism appear more as criticisms of *the division of labour* in a developed capitalist industrial economy. A glimpse of life in a communist society is given by him in a passage in the *German Ideology:*

> For as soon as the division of labour comes into being, each man has a particular, exclusive sphere of activity, which is forced upon him and from which he cannot escape. He is a hunter, a fisherman, a shepherd, or a critical critic, and must remain so if he does not want to lose his means of livelihood; whereas in communist society, where nobody has one exclusive sphere of activity but each can become accomplished in any branch he wishes, society regulates the general production and thus makes it possible for me to do one thing today and another tomorrow, to hunt in the morning, fish in the afternoon, rear cattle in the evening, criticise after dinner, just as I have a mind, without ever becoming hunter, fisherman, shepherd or critic.
>
> (*CW*, Vol 5, p. 47)

Having given a general introduction, we turn in the next chapter to a closer look at the labour theory of value.

Notes to Chapter 1

1. For a perceptive account, see Morishima and Catephores (1978), Ch. 1. Also see Mandel (1971) and McLellan (1973).

2. This is obviously a very brief outline. For fuller and more interesting biographies, see McLellan (1976) and Berlin (1963).
3. See Engels' *Outlines of a Critique of Political Economy* (1843) in *CW*, Vol. 3.
4. See Oakley (1977) for a detailed analysis.
5. Contrast this appreciation with Samuelson's (1962) remark that from 'the point of pure economic theory, Karl Marx can be regarded as a minor post-Ricardian' (p. 12). It is a pity we cannot have more of these minor post-Ricardians and fewer of the minor post-Samuelsons!
6. 'It is impossible completely to understand Marx's *Capital* . . . without having thoroughly studied the *whole* of Hegel's *Logic*' Lenin *Collected Works*, Vol. 38, p. 180.
7. See T. Kuhn's *Structure of Scientific Revolutions* (1970).
8. The usual example is of an arrow in flight. If I shoot an arrow from here, then in some sense it is here, but since it is in motion moving away from me, it is not here.
9. See *Poverty of Philosophy, CW*, Vol. 5, pp. 163—6. Also see *German Ideology, CW*, Vol. 5.
10. See the *Grundrisse*, p. 471 ff.
11. See Sweezy (1942), Ch. 1. Also see Fine and Harris (1979).
12. Although the media is always telling us that class is not important in society, sociologists have found it a useful analytical tool. For accounts of class in Britain see, for example, Goldthorpe (1980) and Halsey (1980).

Further Reading for Chapter 1

1. Cornforth (1977a and 1977b)
2. Fine and Harris (1979) Ch. 1
3. McLellan (1973)
4. Marx (1973) *Grundrisse* Foreword and Introduction
5. Rius (1976)
6. Rowthorn (1974a)
7. Sweezy (1942) Ch. 1

But all science would be superfluous if the outward appearance and the essence of things directly coincided.

(*KIII*, Ch. XLVIII, p. 817)

2 The Labour Theory of Value

2.1 Introduction

In this chapter I shall discuss Marx's labour theory of value (LTV) and explain why it plays a crucial role in understanding Marx's economics. The LTV has a long and distinguished pedigree: variants of the LTV were provided by Adam Smith and David Ricardo. However, Marx's LTV was significantly different from that of earlier writers. For Marx, the LTV was an important way of analysing a capitalist economy: a method of moving from the 'appearances' to 'reality'. As a new paradigm it provided an analytical framework that affects one's perceptions of society.[1]

2.2 Terminological Preliminaries

In reading Marx we must be careful in interpreting what he says, as the terminology he uses is quite different from that used in bourgeois (traditional) economics. Nowadays, economists use the terms 'price' and 'value' interchangeably.[2] However, Classical economists (and Marx) distinguished between *use value* and *exchange value*. Use value would be what we now call utility, while exchange value would be like a relative price of a commodity. For Marx, *value* (without a prefix) differs from both 'use value' and 'exchange value'. Marx would say that if two dissimilar commodities exchange for each other, they must have something in common, namely *social* labour must have been expended on them. The *value* (note there is no prefix) of a commodity is determined by the 'socially necessary labour embodied' in it (see below). *Prices of production* (or 'prices' for short) for Marx are *long-run* equilibrium prices, similar to the Classical idea of 'natural prices'. *Market prices* are the fluctuations around the natural prices: market prices are explained by supply and demand. In general, he has little interest in explaining market prices.

2.3 The Three Systems

In my interpretation of Marx's economics I shall stress the importance of distinguishing three domains: the *commodity* (*physical*) *domain*, the *value domain*, and the *price domain*. We can analyse economic relationships in terms of any one (or all three) of these domains. The *commodity domain* is observable and consists of analysing economic relations in terms of *heterogeneous* commodities. In this domain we would study, for example, technological relationships between inputs and outputs (the 'production function'). Units of measurement would differ from commodity to commodity, e.g., tons of iron, yards of linen, etc. Marx analyses economic relationships mainly in the *value domain*. By using the LTV he aggregates heterogeneous commodities in terms of labour embodied. The value domain is purely an *analytic* construct and is unobservable. All commodities can be reduced to 'abstract labour' and economic relationships can be analysed in terms of values to go beyond the 'appearances' to the 'essence' or 'reality' of things. The units of measurement are units of abstract labour time. The *price domain* consists of market relations where the cash nexus reduces everything to money terms: units of measurement are (say) pounds sterling (£). This is at a level where we can observe the relations between people and things. (Marx argues that a study of economic relations in the price domain is 'superficial' and this is one of the defects of bourgeois economic analysis). Thus in the price domain we would study 'prices of production', profits, wages, etc. Evaluating everything in terms of 'prices of production' we can aggregate heterogeneous commodities. In recent years a controversy has raged over the impossibility of aggregating capital in the price domain and then using this aggregate to determine income distribution by the marginal productivity theory. The Cambridge (England) economists (the so called neo-Ricardians) demonstrated the inconsistency of this procedure, and Cambridge (Massachusetts) (i.e. the neo-Classicals) admitted their 'error'. Although we shall not be entering into that controversy, it is interesting that the analytic problems that Ricardo and Marx were trying to overcome by using the labour theory of value were raised again in the context of neo-Classical capital theory. For an interesting review of this controversy, readers are recommended to look at Harcourt and Laing (1971).

A summary table provides a useful guide:

Table 2.1 The Three Systems

Commodity domain	*Value domain*	*Price domain*
Observable	Non-observable	Non-observable at 'prices of production,
Concrete	Analytic/abstract	Observable at market prices
Units: various	Units: labour time	Concrete?
Production functions/ technological relationships	Social relations	Analytic?
		Units: £'s
		Market relations

An interesting question, to which we shall return in Chapter 3, is to what extent we can move from one domain of our analysis to another. Another interesting question is to what extent we can simply move from the commodity domain to the price domain, *without going through the value domain analysis*. These are all issues that are considered under the heading of the 'transformation problem'. Most of Volume 1 of *Capital* is in the value domain, although Marx often 'converts' the values into pounds sterling. It is crucial to an understanding of Marx's economics that, for example, wages in the value domain may go *down*, while in the commodity domain they remain constant. Similarly, wages in the value domain may be constant, while they *rise* in the price domain. Again, the quantity of commodity X required to produce commodity Y (in the commodity domain) may remain constant, while in the value *domain* the *value* of X required may *fall*.

2.4 Emergence of the Capitalist System of Production

At the heart of the development of a capitalist society lies the development of *production for exchange*. In pre-capitalist societies a large proportion of production is for self-consumption. Any excess over self-consumption is then exchanged for certain essential commodities like clothes, shoes, etc. As society progresses, and the productive potential of society increases, at a certain point producers have a surplus of production over their needs (consumption). At this point, production becomes oriented towards the market: production for exchange has replaced production for use.

In recent years a great debate has raged about the 'periodisation of history': is it possible to delineate epochs in history? What determines the different epochs and the *transition* between epochs? Is there a unilinear progress of epochs? Is it possible for there to be a 'retrogression'? Is it possible to miss out 'stages' in this progress of history? Is it possible for *two* modes of production to coexist in a society? Does the class struggle change the mode of production, or does the mode of production change the class struggle? Modern Marxist historians accept the basic analytical structure of historical materialism, but provide subtle and interesting analyses of European and Asian history. Marx's analysis of pre-capitalist economic formations is contained in diverse places: mainly in *German Ideology* and in *Grundrisse*. However, as neither of these were prepared for publication, nor published in his lifetime, we do not have a clearly presented analysis of the emergence of capitalism. We do have various analytical insights which have been used to study the development of capitalism. I shall not be reviewing the literature on pre-capitalist economic formations. I shall briefly discuss the emergence of capitalism from feudalism in the next few paragraphs.[3]

Marxists (e.g., Dobb, Hobsbawm) would argue against a simple unilinear view of history, although they would accept the basic premises that the 'mode of production' determines the 'relations of production' and that there are epochs in history that have characteristics that are distinctive from preceding ones. It is possible for elements from preceding and succeeding epochs to co-exist in society: a proper analysis of a particular society requires an historical analysis of that particular society. Marx, at times, seems to have a view that *technology* determines the mode of production, and that the mode of production determines the relations of production. We would then need a theory that explains technological change: thus a contradiction between the mode of production and the relations of production could be resolved by a change in technology which would change the mode of production and hence change the relations of production.

To explain the development of capitalism from a feudal economy, we need to explain what led to a decline of feudalism and what led to the rise of capitalism. Before we do that, let me follow Marx's analysis of the importance of the division of labour. Marx begins with the premise that what distinguishes man from other animals is his ability to *produce* his means of subsistence. As man is a social animal we begin to have a social division of labour. As the productive forces of an economy develop (i.e. as technology improves) we have changes in the division of labour, which determine forms of property (mode of production) and the relations of production. 'The various stages in the division of labour are just so many different forms of property . . .' (*German Ideology, CW* Vol. 5, p. 32). Division of labour in pre-capitalist society leads to a separation of town and country, correspondingly a separation between manufacturing and agricultural activities. Initially, exchange takes place simply to satisfy certain needs e.g., farmers need clothes, and weavers need food: this is 'production for use'. At the same time we have the division of labour leading to a separation of mental and physical labour: the development of towns leads to the development of administration, police, tax collectors, local politicians, etc. The separation of town and country is also the separation of landed property and capital independent of land. The development of trade between towns is facilitated by the use of money and the growth of a merchant class. The development of trade between towns also helps communications in general and leads to the spread of knowledge and techniques of production: technology does not have to be re-invented at different times and places.

The decline of feudalism can be explained by its 'inner contradictions' and the rise of capitalism by the growth of world trade and the discovery (by the Europeans) of new countries like America. The development of feudalism showed up the 'inefficiency' of feudal agricultural production: falling productivity coupled with increasing population led to a decline in the surplus. The needs of the ruling classes to finance wars put a strain on the agricultural sector. The runaway serfs found a haven in towns, but the towns were organised on a guild basis. The rural social structure that allows the 'freeing' of the peasantry provides one of the causes of the decline of feudalism. The growth of urban craft commodity production, together with the growth of trade between towns and the growth of world trade, led to 'production for exchange'. The growth of this led to the accumulation of *money capital* which provided the beginnings of capitalist production.

Let me now turn to some key elements of a capitalist system of production:

(a) *Commodities*

These are goods that are for *exchange*, not for personal consumption. Thus if I grow tomatoes to eat with my dinner, then the tomatoes are not a commodity. If I grow tomatoes and sell them in the market-place, then they are a commodity. If I spend several hours producing a 'thing' that no one wants to buy, then that thing is not a commodity. Again, a thing can have use value without being a commodity e.g., air. A commodity must thus have both a use value and an exchange value (see below, Section 2.5).

(b) *Emergence of 'Free' Labour*

In feudal, pre-capitalist society there was no free movement of labour. The social and institutional relationships tied agricultural labour (serfs) to a particular landlord. Similarly, the guild system in towns limited the mobility of labour. With the emergence of capitalism, restrictions on the mobility of labour were lifted and the worker was free to move to the employer who paid the highest wage. At the same time as this freedom, the worker is made 'free of' property: he is dispossessed. The peasant farmer disappears in the enclosure movement in Britain, so that labour is forced to look for work in the industrial capitalist sector. As Marx says:[4]

> Free labourers, in the double sense that neither they themselves form part and parcel of the means of production, as in the case of slaves, bondsmen, &c., nor do the means of production belong to them, as in the case of peasant-proprietors; they are, therefore, free from, unencumbered by, any means of production of their own
>
> (*KI*, Ch. XXVI, p. 714)

As Marx says, nature does not create owners of means of production and workers without any means of production: that is purely a *social* relationship. A study of history shows us changes in the legal forms of property.

(c) *Undifferentiated labour*

During the emergence and development of capitalist production the tasks that labour has to do are simplified, the skilled artisans are replaced by unskilled factory workers. Thus labour required in capitalist production becomes homogeneous, 'abstract labour'. It is clearly a simplification to say that *all* the labour required for production is unskilled homogeneous labour. Homogeneous labour, for Marx, is both a simplifying assumption and the resultant of an historical process.

(d) *Labour Power*

In a capitalist society workers who have been made 'free' have to sell their labour services to capitalists. The worker sells his *labour power* (his *potential* labour services): labour power has become a commodity and just like any other commodity it has use value to the capitalist and exchange value. It is important to note that labour power is a 'perishable' commodity: if it is not sold this week it has disappeared into the past! It is also a perishable commodity in the sense that if it does not manage to sell, it (the worker) will perish! Because the worker has been made free of property, he must sell his labour power for survival. Thus compared to the capitalist, he is in a weak bargaining position.[5] The historical basis of labour power as a commodity is commented upon by Marx:

> Nature does not produce on the one side owners of money or commodities, and on the other men possessing nothing but their own labour-power. This relation has no natural basis, neither is its social basis one that is common to all historical periods.
>
> (*KI*, Ch. VI, p. 169)

(e) *Money*

In the process of development, *one* particular commodity acquires the property of being universally acceptable by social convention. The value of all commodities can be expressed in terms of this 'universal equivalent' — money. The most common form of commodity money is gold, and Marx assumes that gold is money. Money, for Marx, is a unit of account, a medium of exchange, *and a store of value*. This latter function of money plays an important role in Marx's analysis of capitalism. It is curious that this role of money was ignored until its rediscovery by Keynes. (See Chapter 7.)

(f) *From Simple Commodity Production to Capitalist Production*

Simple commodity production (or pre-capitalist production) mainly consists in taking commodities to the market and obtaining money for them, and then using that money to buy other commodities. Note that this is *not* a barter economy. In simple commodity production, money plays an intermediary role. Assuming no cheating, the value of the commodity sold is equal to the value of the commodity bought. This process of the circulation of commodities can be presented schematically as:

$$\hat{C}(C) \rightarrow M(C) \rightarrow \hat{C}(C)$$

where $\hat{C}(C)$ are commodities that are exchanged for money, $M(C)$, and then money is exchanged for other commodities. *I shall use parentheses to indicate in which domain these variables are being measured*. Thus $\hat{C}(C)$ refers to commodities in the commodity domain and $M(C)$ refers to money in the commodity domain. Here 'gold' is being used as money. The *circulation of commodities* begins with a sale and ends with a purchase. But, of course, for each seller there must be a buyer. In this form of commodity production I may go to the market and sell cloth and *then* buy food. The object of commodity production is *production for use*: I produce in order to obtain *use values*. An *alternate* schematic presentation is as follows:

$$\hat{C}(V) \rightarrow M(V) \rightarrow \hat{C}(V)$$

where $\hat{C}(V)$ are commodities measured in the *value domain* and $M(V)$ is money measured in the value domain. Although I purchase a different use value, the value embodied in the purchase equals the value embodied in the sale, assuming there is no cheating.

Under capitalist production when *labour power* has become a commodity, workers go through the same process. They sell their labour power for money and *then* buy commodities. This can be represented in the commodity domain as

$$L(C) \rightarrow M(C) \rightarrow \hat{C}(C)$$

where $L(C)$ is labour power in the commodity domain.

In a capitalist society, where *production is for exchange*, the capitalist begins with an amount of money with which he purchases raw materials and labour power. He produces commodities which he sells for money. This is represented as

$$M(C) \rightarrow \hat{C}(C) \rightarrow M'(C)$$

or $M(V) \rightarrow \hat{C}(V) \rightarrow M'(V)$

where $M'(C)$ is greater than $M(C)$, and $M'(V)$ is greater than $M(V)$. It is clear[6] that the capitalist would not be interested in exchange unless he ends up with M' greater than M. The excess of M' over M, Marx calls surplus value. (See Section 2.6 below.) The capitalist does not spend his money, he merely *advances* it. The question that Marx poses is why is $M' > M$? He has assumed competition and no cheating — what has enabled the capitalist to advance money and receive a surplus? Where did the surplus come from? He argues (see Section 2.6) that the surplus does not arise from the 'circulation of commodities', but from the process of production.

(g) *Emergence of a Capitalist Class*

The capitalists have a class monopoly of the means of production, the workers having been dispossessed. Their sole aim is accumulation and the expansion of wealth. The capitalist is not interested in use values, but only in exchange values, in increasing profits. 'The restless never-ending process of profit making alone is what he aims at . . .' (*KI*, Ch. IV. pp. 152–3).

(h) *The 'Veiling' of Exploitation*

In slave and feudal societies exploitation was obvious, undisguised, open. The slave simply worked for his master in return for only food and shelter. The serf had to provide a certain amount of labour power to the landlord. But under capitalism, labour is free and is *apparently* exchanging on an equal footing with the capitalist, but there is still exploitation. Thus, in spite of freedom of competition, exploitation takes place: exploitation is 'mystified' by market relations, and it is Marx's purpose to expose the 'reality' beneath the 'appearances' (see below).

(i) *Commodity Fetishism*

Under capitalism, *social* relations (between classes) are treated as relations between *things*. Labour power becomes a commodity, a thing, that is traded on the market. Capitalists buy commodities (including labour power) on the market. They 'apparently' deal with 'things', when in fact they are dealing with *social* relationships. The 'appearances' are of competition, of impersonal (democratic?) commodities, while the 'reality' is one of unequal relationships between classes. To quote Marx:

> There is a definite social relation between men, that assumes, in their eyes, the fantastic form of a relation between things
>
> (*KI*, Ch. I., p. 72)

Here Marx is arguing that social relations assume a form which is a 'mental image' ('fantastic' as derived from 'fantasy', or 'phantasy'). Again we see the importance Marx places on the difference between 'reality' and the forms it may take: the 'appearances'. This 'distortion' of social relations is commented on by Marx:

> In capital-profit, or still better capital-interest, land-rent, labour-wages, in this economic trinity represented as the connection between the component parts of value and wealth in general and its sources, we have the complete mystification of the capitalist mode of production, the conversion of social relations into things, the direct coalescence of the material production relations with their historical and social determination. It is an enchanted, perverted, topsy-turvy world, in which Monsieur le Capital and Madame la Terre do their ghost-walking as social characters and at the same time directly as mere things.
>
> (*KIII*, Ch. XLVIII, p. 830)

(j) *Alienation*[7]

Marx has extended discussion on alienation ('estrangement') in the *Economic and Philosophic Manuscripts of 1844*. Although he does not have separate chapters in *Capital* on alienation, the concept is used in the analysis of a capitalist society. Although Marx pays greatest attention to the alienation of the worker, the concept refers to alienation of *man* (including capitalists). Man is alienated (estranged/separated) from (i) his work, (ii) his own products, (iii) his fellow men and (iv) his species.

(i) *Alienation from his work*: in a capitalist society a worker has little control over his work: he is coerced to work, he does not choose what or how to produce. In working, man does not fulfil himself, but degrades himself. With the development and extension of the division of labour, the worker is forced to do routine and repetitious acts which do not give him any satisfaction in his work. Under capitalism a worker's health and physique is attacked by industrial diseases and malformations caused by working in, say, mines. He is mentally degraded by the repetitious and trivial activities performed in factories.

(ii) *Alienation from his own products*: labour's product 'confronts it as *something alien*, as a *power independent* of the producer . . . Under these economic conditions this realisation of labour appears as a *loss of realisation* for the workers; objectification as *loss of the object and bondage to it*; appropriation as *estrangement*, as alienation' (*Economic and Philosophic Manuscripts, CW* Vol. 3, p. 272). The products of labour begin to dominate the worker, he produces commodities, but he cannot consume them. The exchange of commodities, which mask the social relations that underlie them, dominates the worker.

> The worker puts his life into the object; but now his life no longer belongs to him but to the object. Hence, the greater this activity, the more the worker lacks objects. Whatever the product of his labour is, he is not. Therefore the greater this product, the less is he himself. The *alienation* of the worker in his product means not only that his labour becomes an object, an *external* existence, but that it exists *outside him*, independently, as something alien to him, and that it becomes a power on its own confronting him. It means that the life which he has conferred on the object confronts him as something hostile and alien.
> (*Economic and Philosophic Manuscripts, CW* Vol. 3, p. 272, emphasis in original)

(iii) *Alienation from his fellow men*: in a capitalist society the worker is alienated from the capitalist who dominates. The worker has been alienated from his work: by whom? By the capitalist! The worker has been alienated from his products: by whom? By the capitalist!

By the same logic, if the workers are alienated from the capitalist, the *capitalist is alienated from the workers*. The capitalist in his greed for accumulation is also 'dehumanised'.

(iv) *Alienation from his species*: in alienating himself from his work, from his own products, and from his fellow men he is, in effect, alienating himself from man as a species. He is, in effect, becoming a mere animal.

The dehumanising nature of capitalist production is often remarked upon by Marx in various places in *Capital*, but a paragraph from the *Economic and Philosophic Manuscripts* provides a good summary:

> *Political economy conceals the estrangement inherent in the nature of labour by not considering the* **direct** *relationship between the* **worker** (labour) *and production*. It is true that labour produces wonderful things for the rich — but for the worker it produces privation. It produces palaces — but for the worker, hovels. It produces beauty — but

> for the worker, deformity. It replaces labour by machines, but it throws one section of the workers back to a barbarous type of labour, and it turns the other section into a machine. It produces intelligence — but for the worker, stupidity, cretinism.
>
> (*CW* Vol. 3, p. 273, emphasis in original)

The concept of alienation has been discussed in recent years by sociologists, industrial relations 'experts', and by the media. Many of us have heard of, or had the misfortune of possessing, a 'Monday Car' produced by alienated workers. A Swedish car firm, in an attempt to overcome alienation, experimented with small groups of workers producing *entire* cars, so as to give workers 'fulfilment' in their work. They forgot, however, that this was only *one* aspect of alienation!

It is important to note that alienation has nothing whatsoever to do with being paid low wages. As Marx says, '*A forcing up of wages* . . . would therefore be nothing but better *payment for the slave*, and would not win either for the worker or for labour their human status and dignity' (*Economic and Philosophic Manuscripts*, *CW* Vol. 3, p. 280).

2.5 Value and Exchange Value

In this section I shall first discuss the concepts of 'value', 'exchange value' and 'use value'. As discussed above, in a capitalist society workers sell their labour power to capitalists who produce commodities for exchange. Commodities that are exchanged must have something in common: social labour has been expended in their production. For a commodity to have *value*, social labour must have been expended on it: a brick of gold falling from the sky into my garden has no *value*! If I produce a 'thing' which has no use whatsoever to anyone then, *by definition*, no *social* labour has been expended and *hence* the thing is not a commodity and has no *value*. Thus a necessary, though not sufficient, condition for a 'thing' to have *value* is that it must be a *use value*. A 'thing' that has *use value* does not necessarily have *value*; for example, a stone from my garden may be an excellent paper-weight and has use value, but since no *social* labour was expended in its production *it does not have value*. Similarly, air has use value, but no value. Note that so far we have referred to a commodity having value, or not having value (a one-zero decision): *value* is purely a *qualitative* concept. Commodities have value because *abstract* human labour has been used in their production. When we exchange wine for cloth we do not consider the individual worker's labour, but simply some homogeneous *abstract* labour.

Thus when we exchange (say) one bottle of wine for one yard of cloth, the 'common substance' in the two commodities is *abstract* social labour. *Concrete* labour, on the other hand, is the particular labour on the production of a particular commodity. *Concrete labour produces use values. Abstract labour produces values.* Abstract labour does not mean that labour is 'mythical' or not performed in fact: it simply means we abstract from the particularities of its expenditure. Let me support some of the points made above with some quotations from Marx:

> A use value, or useful article, therefore, has value only because human labour in the abstract has been embodied or materialised in it.
>
> (*KI*, Ch. I, p. 38)

> On the one hand all labour is, speaking physiologically, an expenditure of human labour-power, and in its character of identical *abstract* human labour, it creates and forms the *value* of commodities. On the other hand, all labour is the expenditure of human labour-power in a special form and with a definite aim, and in this, its character of *concrete* useful labour, it produces *use values*.
>
> (*KI*, Ch. I, p. 46, emphasis added)

Let me now turn to a *quantitative* aspect of *value*. Since the 'common substance' in commodities is *abstract* labour, it seems obvious that a *quantitative* measure of value would be a quantitative measure of abstract (homogeneous) labour. We therefore measure value by the amount of labour embodied in a commodity. As Marx puts it:

> We see then that which determines the magnitude of the value of any article is the amount of labour socially necessary, or the labour-time socially necessary for its production. Each individual commodity, in this connection, is to be considered as an average sample of its class. Commodities, therefore, in which equal quantities of labour are embodied, or which can be produced in the same time, have the same value.
>
> (*KI*, Ch. I, p. 39)

> The labour-time socially necessary is that required to produce an article under the normal conditions of production, and with the average degree of skill and intensity prevalent at the time.
>
> (*KI*, Ch. I, p. 39)

> The value of a commodity, therefore, varies directly as the quantity, and inversely as the productiveness of the labour incorporated in it.
>
> (*KI*, Ch. I, p. 40)

Several points raised in these quotations need clarification and emphasis. First, the *magnitude* of value (quantitative aspect) depends on the *amount* of socially necessary labour. This means labour must be homogeneous, or if it is not homogeneous there is a method of 'adding' heterogeneous labour. Secondly, by socially necessary labour is meant the amount of labour necessary under *normal* conditions with the *average* degree of skills *given the technology of the day*. That is, if I am hopeless at carpentry and spend a month making a bookcase, then the amount of *socially* necessary labour is the amount of labour which a reasonably proficient carpenter would spend — say, one day. Similarly, if I use backward technology in constructing the bookcase, e.g. a hand saw instead of an electric saw, then the amount of my labour time expended is not socially necessary. The magnitude of value is measured in terms of current 'costs', *not historical 'costs'*. The obvious units of measurement for the magnitude of value are in terms of units of homogeneous labour time. As labour becomes more productive, the (magnitude of) *value* of a commodity falls *even though use values increase*.

Let me return to the problem of measuring the *magnitude* of value. Let me begin with the assumption of *homogeneous abstract labour*. Further let me assume that output is a function of land and labour only, i.e., no capital goods are required. Further assume that we have a fixed coefficient technology, with constant returns to scale. That is, land and labour must be combined in fixed proportions to produce a unit of output (no joint production) and this production can be replicated at any level of production. By definition, land has no value. Land is simply the 'original and indestructible properties of soil'. The value of output, say corn, is unambiguously defined as the quantity of labour embodied in the product. If the climate is good in any one year, greater *use values* are created, but the amount of *value* is the same from year to year (assuming no technological change). For example, if 1 acre of land and 100 hours of labour produce 10 bushels of corn, then the value of corn is 100 hours of labour time.

Now let me turn to the case of heterogeneous labour in the case discussed above. Assume that the production process is as before, except that two types of labour are required: skilled and unskilled. Assume that in the numerical example that we require 20 hours of skilled labour and 60 hours of unskilled labour. How do we 'add' up these two different types of labour? It should be clear that we cannot use the wage rates of the two types as 'weights', since that would make the value of corn depend on what happens in the *price domain*. Values would not be independent of the price domain, and since

Marx would like to determine prices from values, we would have an element of circularity. Although Marx does not spend much time discussing this issue he seems to think that it has a simple solution. He argues, in effect, that if the differences in skilled and unskilled labour are due not to natural abilities but to training, we can treat skilled labour as a constant multiple of unskilled labour.

> Skilled labour counts only as simple labour intensified, or rather, as multiplied simple labour, a given quantity of skilled being considered equal to a greater quantity of simple labour . . . The different proportions in which different sorts of labour are reduced to unskilled labour as their standard, are established by a social process that goes on behind the backs of the producers, and, consequently, appear to be fixed by custom. For simplicity's sake we shall henceforth account every kind of labour to be unskilled, simple labour; by this we do no more than save ourselves the trouble of making the reduction.
>
> (*KI*, Ch. I, p. 44)

Although there has been a debate in the journals on this issue,[9] I shall move on to the next item on the agenda, viz. *exchange value*. As a preliminary, let me remind the reader of the distinction that Marx draws between 'appearances' and 'reality'. When commodities exchange in the market they have both *use value* and *value*. The manifestation of value in the market, i.e. the *form* value takes in the market place, is exchange value. Thus value is the 'essence' or 'reality', exchange value the 'appearance' or the visible form that value takes. As Marx says, value is 'a relation between persons expressed as a relation between things' (*KI*, Ch. I, p. 74, f.n.1). This returns to the idea of fetishism of commodities. Again, 'exchange value, generally, is only the mode of expression, the phenomenal form, of something contained in it; yet distinguishable from it' (*KI*, Ch. I, p. 37).

A commodity is a use value and a *value*. To quote Marx:

> In other words, the value of a commodity obtains independent and definite expression, by taking the form of exchange-value. When, at the beginning of this chapter, we said, in common parlance, that a commodity is both a use-value and an exchange-value, we were, accurately speaking, wrong. A commodity is a use-value or object of utility, and a value. It manifests itself as this two-fold thing, that it is, as soon as its value assumes an independent form — viz., the form of exchange-value. It never assumes this form when isolated, but only when placed in a value or exchange relation with another commodity of a different kind. When once we know this, such a mode of expression does no harm; it simply serves as an abbreviation.
>
> (*KI*, Ch. I, p. 60)

Exchange value is a quantitative concept, but unlike value must be expressed in terms of some other commodity. Thus we get *several* exchange values for a commodity, e.g., (to use Marx's example):

20 yards of linen = 1 coat
20 yards of linen = 10 lbs of tea
etc.

Thus we compare different types of concrete labour producing different commodities in terms of their abstract labour: in terms of their value. Marx argues that *value* is the 'essence' and exchange value the 'appearance'. Thus to understand and explain exchange values we must first understand and explain *value*. In his words:

> It becomes plain, that it is not the exchange of commodities which regulates the magnitude of their value; but, on the contrary, that it is the magnitude of their value *which controls their exchange proportions.*
> (*KI*, Ch. I, p. 63, emphasis added)

It is important to note that Marx is saying that exchange values are *determined* by values, not that they are *proportional* to values. Marx seems to use the term *relative value* in almost exactly the same way as exchange value. For example, if we look at the relative value of *A* compared to *B*, then if the *value* of *B* falls, the relative value (exchange value) of *A* has risen. If the values of *A and B* change in the same proportion, then the relative value of *A* is constant. At a certain stage all exchange values are expressed in terms of *one* particular commodity which becomes the 'universal equivalent'. This universal equivalent is the money commodity: gold. The relative value of a commodity in terms of this universal equivalent (money) is the 'price form of that commodity' (*KI*, Ch. I, p. 70). Thus, if 20 yards of linen = 2 ounces of gold and when coined 2 ounces of gold = £2, then 20 yards of linen = £2. (This illustration is from *KI*, p. 70.) Let me end this discussion with a quotation from *Contribution to a Critique of Political Economy*:

> Since the exchange-value of commodities is indeed nothing but a mutual relation between various kinds of labour of individuals regarded as equal and universal labour, *i.e.*, nothing but a material expression of a specific social form of labour, *it is a tautology to say that labour is the only source of exchange-value* and accordingly of wealth in so far as this consists of exchange-value. It is equally a tautology to say that material in its natural state does not have exchange-value since it contains no labour, and that exchange-value as such includes no material in a natural state.
> (p. 35, emphasis added)

Let me summarise the discussion so far. Commodities have use value and value. Value has a qualitative and a quantitative dimension. The magnitude of value is measured in units of abstract (homogeneous) labour time. The *form* value takes in circulation is exchange value. Exchange value is a relative concept, but may be measured in terms of a universal equivalent, money. The money form of exchange value is the price of a commodity. Exchange value is determined by (the magnitude of) value.

It is important to note that value is predicated on the circulation of commodities, but *its magnitude is assumed to be independent of circulation*. Put in bourgeois terminology, the *magnitude* of value is independent of demand and supply. It is determined by social and technological relationships. (Note that for a commodity to have *value* there must be a demand for it, but the extent of the demand does not affect its magnitude). It is curious to note that in a passage in *Capital* Marx appears to argue that if the supply of a commodity exceeds demand, then *too much* social labour has been expended on it. But this makes the magnitude of value depend upon market relations in the price domain. In his words:

> Lastly, suppose that every piece of linen in the market contains no more labour-time than is socially necessary. In spite of this, all these pieces taken as a whole, may have had superfluous labour-time spent upon them. If the market cannot stomach the whole quantity at the normal price of 2 shillings a yard, this proves that too great a portion of the total labour of the community has been expended in the form of weaving. The effect is as if each individual weaver had expended more labour-time upon his particular product than is socially necessary.
>
> (*KI*, Ch. III, p. 107)

2.6 Surplus Value

The origin, nature and distribution of surplus value play a crucial role in Marx's analysis. Capitalists and workers meet on 'apparent' equal terms in the 'free market' and the workers sell their labour *power* to the capitalist. The capitalist pays the worker according to the value of labour power. The value of labour power (which in a capitalist economy is just like any other commodity) is determined by the amount of socially necessary labour embodied in it (the labour power). The value of labour power is the amount of socially necessary labour embodied in the commodities the worker must consume to produce and reproduce himself. The capitalist pays according to the exchange value, but obtains the *use value* of the labour power. This distinction between use value and value (or exchange value) of labour power is fundamental to an understanding of the concept of surplus value. Labour power is a peculiar commodity in that the value it creates is in excess of its own value.

As I explained above, capitalist production is for exchange, that is, capitalists produce commodities (which by definition must be use values to someone) in order to sell them to 'expand' their capital: to increase profits. What is it that allows capitalists to make profits, in a *competitive* system, as a norm? Marx is trying to explain the existence of profits in aggregate. Thus if one capitalist makes a profit at the expense of another capitalist by indulging in sharp practices, one man's gain is another man's loss: it is a zero-sum game. In aggregate, circulation cannot explain the existence of profits.

> Turn and twist as we may, the fact remains unaltered. If equivalents are exchanged, no surplus value results, and if non-equivalents are exchanged, still no surplus-value. Circulation, or the exchange of commodities, begets no value.
>
> (*KI*, Ch. V, p. 163)

The existence of surplus value comes from the existence of a unique commodity, labour power:

> In order to be able to extract value from the consumption of a commodity, our friend, Moneybags [the capitalist], must be so lucky as to find, within the sphere of circulation, in the market, a commodity, whose use value possesses the peculiar property of being a source of value, whose actual consumption, therefore, is itself an embodiment of labour, and consequently a creation of value.
>
> (*KI*, Ch. IV, p. 167, square brackets added).

The value of labour power is determined by the value of commodities in the subsistence basket required for the maintenance of the worker and the means for reproducing more workers.

> The value of labour-power resolves itself into the value of a definite quantity of the means of subsistence. It therefore varies with the value of these means or with the quantity of labour requisite for their production.
>
> (*KI*, Ch. VI, p. 172.)

Also, these means of subsistence must include 'the means necessary for the labourer's substitutes, i.e., his children, in order that this race of peculiar commodity-owners may perpetuate its appearance in the market' (*KI*, Ch. VI, p. 172).

For educated skilled labour we must add the costs of education in terms of the value of commodities. 'The expenses of education, enter *pro tanto* into the total value spent in its production' (*KI*, Ch. VI, p. 172).

Unlike other commodities, the value of labour power has a 'moral' and social element in it which would vary from country to country and over time.

> In contradistinction therefore to the case of other commodities, there enters into the determination of the value of labour-power a historical and moral element. Nevertheless, in a given country, at a given period, the average quantity of the means of subsistence necessary for the labourer is practically known.
>
> (*KI*, Ch. VI, p. 171)

It is important to note that the subsistence level is *not* a physical minimum. It increases over time due to the increasing prosperity of society. The 'moral' and 'historical' element has been mentioned above. Marx is equally explicit that it is not a *physical* minimum.

> The *minimum* limit of the value of labour-power is determined by the value of the commodities, without the daily supply of which the labourer cannot renew his vital energy, consequently by the value of those means of subsistence that are *physically* indispensable. *If the price of labour-power falls to this minimum, it falls below its value, since under such circumstances it can be maintained and developed only in a crippled state.* But the value of every commodity is determined by the labour-time requisite to turn it out so as to be of normal quality.
>
> (*KI*, Ch. VI, p. 173, emphasis added).

Let me illustrate the concept of value of labour power with a numerical example. Assume that a worker requires (needs) one loaf of bread and one pound of meat a day to have adequate energy to work efficiently and to be able to survive long enough to produce healthy children. I am ignoring (for simplicity) all the other commodities that realistically should be included, e.g., housing, electricity, heating, clothing, etc. Assume that it takes four hours of abstract labour time to produce one pound of meat and one hour of abstract labour time to produce one loaf. Further assume that the price of meat is £1.60 per pound, and bread is 40p a loaf. Finally, assume that five hours of abstract labour produce 1 ounce of gold, which sells at £2.00. This can be illustrated in tabular form (all on a daily basis), thus:

Table 2.2 The Value of Labour Power

Value Domain (£'s)	*Value Domain (units of labour time)*	*Commodity Domain*	*Price (£'s)*	*Domain*
1.60	4 hours	1 lb meat	1.60 × 1 =	1.60
0.40	1 hour	1 loaf	0.40 × 1 =	0.40
£2.00	5 hours per day)	? (per day)		£2.00 (per day)

The subsistence commodity bundle for the worker is 1 lb meat and 1 loaf per day (which we cannot add together because they are *different*) and the *value* of labour power (measured in labour time) is 5 hours per day. If the prices of commodities are as assumed, then the worker must have a wage in the *price domain* of £2.00 per day. Marx often converts values into *money units* by finding out how much labour is embodied into 1 ounce of gold, and then uses the price of gold to convert labour units into money units. In our illustration, 5 hours produce 1 oz of gold worth £2.00, that is, 1 hour produces gold worth £2.00/5 = 0.40p. Therefore, 5 hours of labour time can be expressed as £2.00. It is important to note that this is a *simplification that he makes in the analysis in Volumes 1 and 2 of* Capital. In the next chapter I shall discuss the so-called 'transformation problem' of converting values into prices. Let me assume that I can convert values in terms of labour time into values in terms of money units.[10]

So far in the analysis everything is above board and the capitalist pays the worker the value of his labour power, £2.00 per day. The worker's labour power is now (temporarily) the property of the capitalist. Marx's description of this is graphic and deserves quotation in full:

> The consumption of labour-power is completed, as in the case of every other commodity, outside the limits of the market or of the sphere of circulation. Accompanied by Mr. Moneybags and by the possessor of labour-power, we therefore take leave for a time of this noisy sphere, where everything takes place on the surface and in view of all men, and follow them both into the hidden abode of production, on whose threshold there stares us in the face 'No admittance except on business'. Here we shall see, not only how capital produces, but how capital is produced. We shall at last force the secret of profit making.
>
> This sphere that we are deserting, within those boundaries the sale and purchase of labour-power goes on, is in fact a very Eden of the innate

> rights of man. There alone rule Freedom, Equality, Property and Bentham. Freedom, because both buyer and seller of a commodity, say of labour-power, are constrained only by their own free will. They contract as free agents, and the agreement they come to, is but the form in which they give legal expression to their common will. Equality, because each enters into relation with the other, as with a simple owner of commodities, and they exchange equivalent for equivalent. Property, because each disposes only of what is his own. And Bentham, because each looks only to himself. The only force that brings them together and puts them in relation with each other, is the selfishness, the gain and the private interests of each. Each looks to himself only, and no one troubles himself about the rest, and just because they do so, do they all, in accordance with the pre-established harmony of things, or under the auspices of an all-shrewd providence, work together to their mutual advantage, for the common weal and in the interest of all.
>
> On leaving this sphere of simple circulation or of exchange of commodities, which furnishes the 'Free-trader Vulgaris' with his views and ideas, and with the standard by which he judges a society based on capital and wages, we think we can perceive a change in the physiognomy of our dramatis personae. He, who before was the money-owner, now strides in front as capitalist; the possessor of labour-power follows as his labourer. The one with an air of importance, smirking, intent on business; the other timid and holding back, like one who is bringing his own hide to market and has nothing to expect but — a hiding.
>
> (*KI*, Ch. VI, pp. 175–6)

Let me highlight and emphasise one of the points Marx is making above. Relations in the sphere of circulation (exchange) are apparently on an equal footing, but this is a *superficial* account. Until we study the process of the creation of surplus value in the *production* sphere, we cannot observe and analyse the unequal relations between labour and capital. This is the criticism he makes, and Marxists make, of bourgeois economists: they study only the superficial market (exchange) relations and do not penetrate to the 'essence' or 'reality'.

Let me return to the creation of surplus value. The worker has sold his labour power to the capitalist at its value. The capitalist now has (temporary) control over the worker's labour power. The worker, in the production process, has lost his freedom: he must do what the capitalist commands. The capitalist would control the worker so that he works in an efficient way so that he produces as much as possible using as little of inputs (raw materials) and with due care and attention to the machinery. The products of labour are the property of the capitalist. The capitalist having paid the exchange value of labour power has gained its *use value. Let me now assume for illustrative purposes that the capitalist is producing 'food' with a given* amount of land. The value of labour power is determined by the amount of socially necessary labour embodied in the amount of 'food' required for subsistence, i.e., 5 hours of labour time. Once the capitalist has bought the labour power, he makes the worker work a 10 hour day. In effect, the worker is working for 5 hours to feed himself and 5 hours for the capitalist *without recompense*. Let me show this diagrammatically in Diagram 2.1.

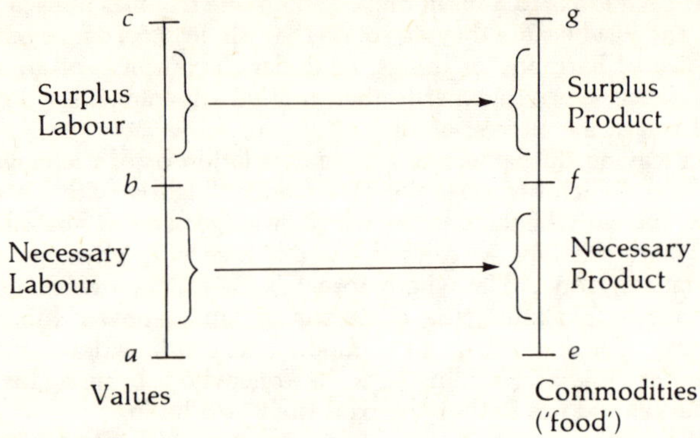

Diagram 2.1 *Necessary and Surplus Labour*

In 5 hours' labour time (*ab*) he produces 'food' equal to *ef* and in the remaining part of the working day (*bc*) he produces *fg* amount of 'food'. The capitalist has paid a wage equal to the value of labour power which enables the worker to buy back sufficient commodities for subsistence. In the remainder of the day he works *gratis* for the capitalist! In general, the worker produces commodities he does not consume, so that we have first to find out the value of labour power, then find out the wage he receives with which he can buy his subsistence bundle of goods. This is illustrated in Diagram 2.2.

The actual process is more complicated than the one represented above, since I had (by assumption) ignored raw materials and machinery. The capitalist begins with money capital with which he buys raw materials and labour power.

2.7 Constant and Variable Capital

Marx distinguishes between *constant capital* and *variable capital*. Constant capital includes raw materials and machinery. They are

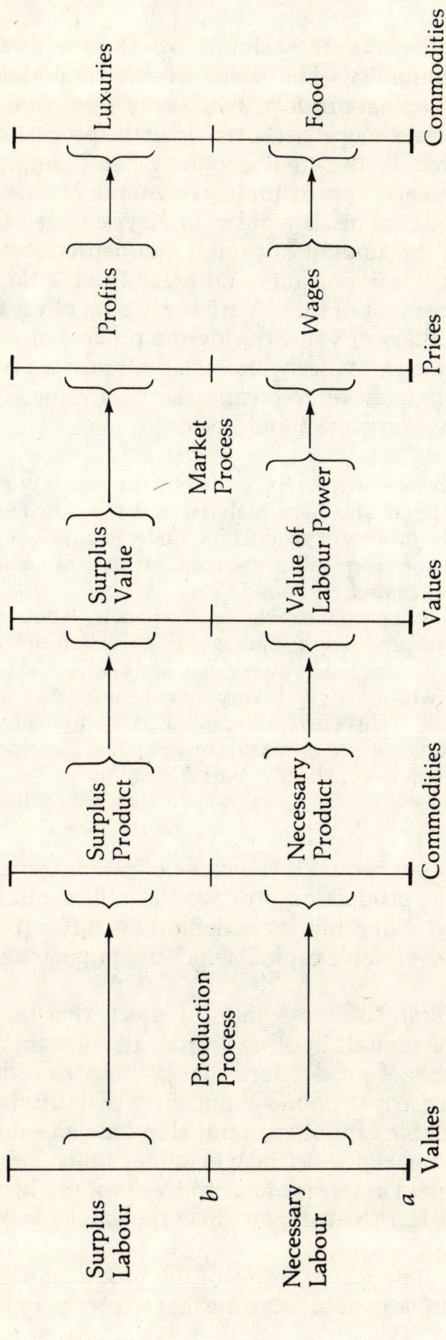

Diagram 2.2 *The Labour Theory of Value*

called *constant* capital because they simply *transfer* their value to the final product commodity. The value of raw materials gets transferred in full to the final product, while only a *fraction* of the value of fixed capital (machinery) gets used up in the process of production and transferred to the final product. For example, if a machine 'lives' for ten years, approximately one-tenth of it gets used up (worn out) each year. This is similar to Keynes' user cost of capital which refers to the amount of capital that depreciates in the process of production. It is important to note that this is a *flow* concept, x units of value per unit of time. Variable capital refers to that part of capital which alters in value during the process of production, namely, labour power. As seen above, labour power produces value to replace itself in addition to creating surplus value. The exact definitions used by Marx are quoted below:

> That part of capital then, which is represented by the means of production, by the raw material, auxiliary material and the instruments of labour, does not, in the process of production, undergo any quantitative alteration of value. I therefore call it the constant part of capital, or, more shortly, *constant capital*.
>
> On the other hand, that part of capital, represented by labour-power, does, in the process of production, undergo an alteration of value. It both reproduces the equivalent of its own value, and also produces an excess, a surplus-value, which may itself vary, may be more or less according to circumstances. This part of capital is continually being transformed from a constant into a variable magnitude. I therefore call it the variable part of capital, or, shortly, *variable capital*.
>
> (*KI*, Ch. VIII, p. 209)

To summarise, constant capital is the value of raw materials and machines used up in the production process. Variable capital is the value of labour power. Note that these definitions differ from the terms 'fixed capital' and 'variable capital' which are popular amongst bourgeois economists.

In Volume I of *Capital*, Marx assumes, in effect, that there is a unit turnover period of capital. In other words, all constant capital is used up in the process of production, that is there is no durable capital. Let me emphasise two points about these definitions: first, both constant and variable capital are defined in the *value* domain, although Marx sometimes expresses them in money units. Secondly, constant capital is defined in terms of *current* values, not historical values. Thus technological change may affect the value of constant and/or variable capital.

Let me now give a numerical example of the production process with constant and variable capital. Assume that to produce cloth we need raw materials with a value of 50 labour hours, machinery which lasts for ten years with a value of 100 labour hours, and variable capital of 20 labour hours. Further, assume that workers are made to work 40 hours: the capitalist gets the use value of labour power. The value of the commodity produced is $(50 + 10) + 40 = 100$ labour hours. The capitalist, in the market, bought constant capital and variable capital at its value. Nevertheless, he has produced surplus value: $100 - (50 + 10 + 20) = 20$ labour hours. As mentioned earlier, all these values could be converted into money units as Marx does in his illustrations. Thus surplus value arises with free markets and competition. In Marx's words:

> Every condition of the problem is satisfied, while the laws that regulate the exchange of commodities, have been in no way violated. Equivalent has been exchanged for equivalent. For the capitalist as buyer paid for each commodity, for the cotton, the spindle and the labour-power, its full value. He then did what is done by every purchaser of commodities; he consumed their use value . . . This metamorphosis, this conversion of money into capital, takes place both within the sphere of circulation and also outside it; within the circulation, because conditioned by the purchase of the labour-power in the market; *outside the circulation, because what is done within it is only a stepping-stone to the production of surplus-value, a process which is entirely confined to the sphere of production.*
>
> (*KI*, Ch. VII, pp. 194–5, emphasis added)

It is important to note that the magnitude of surplus value is *independent* of the amount of constant capital employed in the production process. Constant capital simply transfers values. Inputs like land which have had no labour employed to prepare it for production have, by definition, no value. Land creates *use* values, but not values. Clearly, the use of constant capital is a necessary condition for production. Technical conditions determine the combinations of constant capital and labour power used. Given constant capital it 'may rise or fall in value, or even be, as land and the sea, without any value in itself; but this will have no influence on the creation of value or on the variation in the quantity of value.' (*KI*, Ch. IX, p. 215. Also see *KI*, Ch. XI, p. 306).

To reiterate, surplus value is defined (in the value domain) as the difference between the value of the product and the value of inputs (including labour power) used up in the production process.[11]

2.8 Magnitude of Surplus Value: Absolute and Relative Surplus Value

Given a subsistence *commodity* bundle, surplus value can be increased in one of two ways:

(a) increasing the length of working day (*absolute surplus value*)
(b) decreasing the *value* of labour power, i.e., decreasing necessary labour (*relative surplus value*).

Absolute surplus value can be increased by an extension of the working day, but this depends on the relative strengths of the capitalist class and the working class.

> Hence is it that in the history of capitalist production, the determination of what is a working day, presents itself as the result of a struggle, a struggle between collective capital, i.e., the class of capitalists, and collective labour, i.e., the working class.
>
> (*KI*, Ch. X, p. 235)

Relative surplus value can be increased by decreasing the *value* of labour power. The value of labour power can be decreased by increased labour productivity *in the production of the subsistence commodity bundle* of the worker. Thus, if there is increased productivity in the food producing industry, each unit of food would have less labour embodied in it and hence the subsistence bundle would have a lower value. Note that the worker still consumes the *same* basket of goods, but their value has fallen. Marx argues that it *may* be possible that increasing productivity may allow the worker to *increase* his basket of goods, although this implies the worker is being paid more than his value. (See *KI*, Ch. XVII, p. 523.)

Let us now see the effect of increasing productivity by *one* capitalist in the non-subsistence goods sector. Because the increased productivity is not 'general', the (social) value of the commodity is unchanged, although the *private* value per unit of commodity has fallen. Thus this capitalist still gets the (*social*) value for his commodity which exceeds his *private* value. Hence the innovating capitalist receives a temporary 'excess' surplus value. Competition forces other capitalists to adopt the new method of production, thus leading to a fall in the (social) value of the commodity and hence wiping out the 'excess' surplus value. (This argument is similar to Schumpeter's argument about the innovator who makes excess profits in a dynamic system.) Thus an individual capitalist can increase surplus value by increasing productivity in *any* branch of industry. (See *KI*, Ch. XII, pp. 317–20.)

Increasing 'intensity of labour', that is, more effort being expended in a given period of time, also increases relative surplus value. This argument is analogous to increasing productivity.

2.9 Rate of Surplus Value

The rate of surplus value, or the rate of exploitation, is defined as the ratio of surplus value created to the value of variable capital.

Let me set down some notation:

$c(V)$ = constant capital measured in the value domain
$v(V)$ = variable capital measured in the value domain
$s(V)$ = surplus value measured in the value domain

The rate of surplus value is defined as

$$s'(V) = \frac{\text{surplus value}}{\text{variable capital}} = \frac{\text{surplus value}}{\text{value of labour power}}$$

$$= \frac{\text{surplus labour}}{\text{necessary labour}} = \frac{s(V)}{v(V)}$$

As mentioned earlier, surplus value is measured in the value domain, but is often expressed by Marx in money units. Variable capital is the amount of capital the capitalist needs to hire labour power if he pays the worker his value. By definition, variable capital equals value of labour power. The last part of the equality is in terms of labour time necessary to reproduce his subsistence, and the numerator is the remainder of his working day.

Marx assumes that the rate of exploitation is uniform across all firms and industries. This is because of the assumption of homogeneous labour, a uniform value of labour power, and free mobility of labour. Under competitive conditions, if the rates of exploitation differed, labour would migrate from the high exploitation firms (industries) to the low exploitation firms (industries). Thus competition would give a uniform working day and hence uniform rates of exploitation. This is obviously a simplifying assumption, but one which would be a closer approximation to reality the more developed the capitalist economy. (See *KIII*, Ch. X, p. 175.)

2.10 Productive and Unproductive Labour[12]

In recent years there has been a debate about the nature and extent of productive labour which was sparked off by Baran and Sweezy's *Monopoly Capital* (1966). In this section I shall briefly outline Marx's discussion of these concepts, without getting involved in the controversy, which is peripheral to this book.

In a capitalist economy where production is for exchange, labour power that is used in the production process creates surplus value. Labour that creates surplus value is *productive* labour. Labour used in the process of circulation does not produce surplus value and is therefore *unproductive*. The distinction is independent of whether the commodity is a tangible product like food, or an intangible product like the services of a teacher. The same actions provided by labour may be productive or unproductive, depending on whether the labour is employed to produce surplus or not. Thus, if I teach my children how to read and write in my home, my labour is unproductive. If I am employed by a *private* school to teach children how to read and write, I help to create surplus value for my capitalist employer and hence I am productive. If I am employed in a *State* school I do not produce a 'commodity' and hence I am unproductive.

Again, whether labour is productive or unproductive is independent of whether the commodity produced is 'socially' useful or not. Labour employed by capitalists in the production of cigarettes or cocaine, heroin or hashish, is productive labour.

In addition to the productive/unproductive categories of labour, there is a third category of labour: *non-productive* labour. Thus the labour of self-employed craftsmen or peasant farmers who employ no wage labour is non-productive. They produce *commodities* but *not* in a *capitalist mode of production* and hence their labour is neither productive nor unproductive. This is even though the craftsman or peasant produces more than the value of his labour power, i.e., he produces a surplus value.

Wage labour employed by a capitalist in the transport of commodities to the market is treated as productive labour. Labour employed as salesmen is treated as unproductive labour. In a modern capitalist economy advertising employs many workers who do not fit clearly into Marx's categorisation, although some Marxists treat them as unproductive. Similarly, is the domestic labour provided by a housewife productive or unproductive? Since housewives are not employed as wage labour and do not produce commodities in a capitalist mode of production, they are, by Marx's definitions, unproductive labour.[13]

To summarise, labour employed to produce commodities in a capitalist mode of production produces surplus values and hence is productive labour.

2.11 Organic Composition of Capital

Marx defines the organic composition of capital as the ratio of constant capital to variable capital, both defined in the value domain. Thus

$$q(V) = \frac{c(V)}{v(V)} = \frac{\text{dead labour}}{\text{live labour}}$$

where $q(V)$ is the organic composition of capital (OCC), $c(V)$ is constant capital, and $v(V)$ is variable capital, *all defined in the value domain*. Since constant capital in value terms is simply labour embodied in commodities some time in the past, it is 'dead' labour. Variable capital is labour power currently employed, hence 'live' labour. The ratio of these two values is the organic composition of capital. The ratio of constant capital to variable capital in the *commodity* domain is called the *technical* composition of capital (TCC). Thus:

$$q(C) = \frac{c(C)}{v(C)} = \frac{\text{commodities used as constant capital}}{\text{labour power}}$$

where q, c and v are in the commodity domain. As long as there is only *one* kind of constant capital this ratio is meaningful; with different commodities in constant capital we would need some rules for aggregating the different commodities.

Assuming a single commodity constant capital and no technical change, there would be a one-to-one correspondence between the organic and technical compositions of capital. If technical change is 'neutral', that is, labour productivity in *all* sectors changes proportionately, then there is a simple relation between the TCC and OCC.[14] As there is a controversy about this concept, let me quote Marx's definition:

> The composition of capital is to be understood in a two-fold sense. On the side of value, it is determined by the proportion in which it is divided into constant capital or value of the means of production, and variable capital or value of labour-power, the sum total of wages. On the side of material, as it functions in the process of production, all capital is divided into means of production and living labour-power. This latter composition is determined by the relation between the mass of the means of production employed, on the one hand, and the mass of labour necessary for their employment on the other. I call the former the *value-composition*, the latter the *technical composition* of capital. Between the two there is a strict correlation. To express this, I call the value-composition of capital, in so far as it is determined by its technical composition and mirrors the change of the latter, the *organic composition* of capital.
>
> (*KI*, Ch. XXV, p. 612, emphasis added).

Fine and Harris (1979) distinguish *three* versions of the composition of capital:

(a) *technical composition* of capital (as above);
(b) *organic composition* of capital measured in the *value* domain, but at *historical* values; and

(c) *value composition* of capital (VCC) in the value domain at *current* values.

The significance of these distinctions will become apparent when we turn to discuss the issue of the falling rate of profit in Chapter 6.

2.12 Rate of Profit

Marx defines the rate of profit in the value domain as

$$\pi(V) = \frac{s(V)}{c(V) + v(V)}$$

and dividing the numerator and denominator of the right-hand side by $v(V)$ we get:

$$\pi(V) = \frac{s'(V)}{q(V) + 1}$$

As before, s, c and v are defined in the value domain, but converted into money units by assuming that prices equal value. In fact, as we shall see in the next chapter, s, c and v must be transformed into the price domain to define a rate of profit in the price domain. Competition amongst capitalists leads to an equalisation of the profit rate in the price domain.

2.13 Summary

In this chapter I have discussed some of the basic concepts of Marx's analysis. The main points are that in a capitalist economy commodities are produced for exchange in a competitive market. Labour power is a commodity that is sold to the capitalists at its value. However, the use value of labour power exceeds its value and therefore creates surplus value. Hence, workers are exploited by capitalists. If we study only market relations, exploitation is veiled; it is only when we use the labour theory of value to study the labour process which lies behind market relations that we can get to the 'reality' of a capitalist economy.

Notes to Chapter 2

1. For an interesting methodological account, see Sen (1978).

2. Oscar Wilde defines a cynic as a 'man who knows the price of everything and the value of nothing.' The same could be said of bourgeois economists!
3. See Dobb (1963), Brenner (1978), Hilton (1976) and Hobsbawm (1964).
4. Also see *Grundrisse*, p. 507.
5. See *Grundrisse*, p. 506.
6. See *KI*, Ch. 4.
7. For an excellent discussion, see Ollman (1976). Detailed references to the concept of alienation in *Capital* are contained in the notes to Ollman's book. Also see *Grundrisse*, pp. 459 ff.
8. I am using the term 'capital goods' in the 'bourgeois' economics sense, e.g. machinery.
9. See Rowthorn (1974a) and Fine and Harris (1979).
10. These are what Shaikh (1977) calls 'direct prices'.
11. See *KI*, Ch. VIII, p. 208 for an exact definition.
12. See Morishima (1973) pp. 34–35.
13. See *TSVI*, p. 405, where Marx discusses an analogous case of buying a teacher's service to improve one's skills. These affect the value of labour power, but the teacher's services are unproductive. For an interesting discussion of this subject see Gardiner, Himmelweit and Mackintosh (1975).
14. For a critical discussion see Fine and Harris (1979), Ch. 3. Also see Gough (1972) and Harrison (1973). The most extensive discussion of this topic by Marx is in *TSVI*, Ch. IV and Addenda 12. Discussion in *Capital* is scattered in various places; Gough (1972) has an interesting selection of quotes.

Further Reading for Chapter 2

Section 2.2

1. Marx *Wages, Price and Profit* (1865) in *SWI*

Section 2.3

1. Medio *Profits and Surplus Value . . .*, in Hunt & Schwartz (1972)

Section 2.4

1. Marx & Engels *German Ideology, CW* Vol. 5
2. *KIII* Ch. XLVII
3. Marx *Grundrisse*, pp. 471–514.
4. Marx *Economic & Philosophic Manuscripts* (1844) in *CW* Vol. 3
5. Hobsbawm (1964) Introduction
6. Brenner (1978)
7. Ollman (1976)
8. Mészáros (1975)

Sections 2.5, 2.6, 2.7, 2.8, 2.9

1. *KI* Chs 1–3, 4–9, 12, 16–18
2. *KIII* Chs L, LI

3. Sweezy (1942) Chs 2–4
4. Meek (1973) Chs 4–7 & Introduction
5. Dobb (1973) Ch. 6
6. Sraffa Introduction, in Ricardo (1951)

Section 2.10
1. *TSVI* Ch. IV and Addenda 12
2. Gough (1972)
3. Fine & Harris (1979) Ch. 3

The profit ... is thus the same as surplus value, only in a mystified form that is nonetheless a necessary outgrowth of the capitalist mode of production.

(*KIII*, Ch. 1, p. 36)

3 The Transformation Problem

3.1 Introduction

In the last chapter I discussed the labour theory of value (LTV) and emphasised its importance in analysing the social relationships that underlie the production process. In *KI* Marx analysed capitalist *production* predicated on the *circulation* of commodities (exchange) in a capitalist mode of production. In *KII* Marx analyses the circulation of commodities and *then* in *KIII* he goes on to discuss the *Process of Capitalist Production as a Whole.* In *KI* and *KII* he *assumes* that commodities exchange at their values, so as to analyse the origin and nature of profits in abstract without the 'intruding' influences of competition between different capitalists in the marketplace.[1] The transformation problem, at one level, is to do with the transforming of 'surplus value' into 'profits', from the value domain to the price domain. At another level, it is to do with the transforming of 'values' into 'prices of production'. In *KI* Marx analyses capitalist production in terms of values; if commodities exchange at their values it would imply that profit rates in different departments (sectors) would differ if organic compositions of capital differ. In *KIII* Marx shows how prices of production (long-run equilibrium prices) diverge *systematically* from value. A common, but mistaken, view is that Marx discovered only after he completed *KI* and *KII* that, in general, prices could not be proportional to values and that he tried to correct his 'mistake' in *KIII*. However, it is clear from the *Grundrisse, Theories of Surplus Value* (both written before *KIII*) and a letter to Engels in 1862, that he knew that prices could not be proportional to values and outlined a solution to the problem. In this Chapter I shall first outline the concept of 'Simple Reproduction' in a model of circulation and then go on to discuss the transformation problem as solved by Marx, its shortcomings, and suggested improvements. Finally, I shall assess the role of the LTV in Marx's analysis.

3.2 Simple Reproduction: A Digression

In the previous chapter I presented an exposition of how surplus value is created in the process of capitalist production. The capitalist begins with an amount of money with which he buys commodities (including labour power) and produces commodities whose value is greater than the initial value. Having produced new commodities, he sells them to consumers at *market* prices. As Marx would like to abstract from temporary fluctuations in prices, his analysis is carried out in terms of long-run equilibrium prices. The commodities are assumed to sell at 'prices of production'. In the process the capitalist is able to capture (some of) the surplus value created in the production process. Competition between capitalists ensures that the prices of production that emerge must be such as to have equalised the rate of profit (determined at these equilibrium prices). What are the circumstances under which the economic system can continue these exchange relationships, the circulation process, without an increase or decrease *over all* in the circular flow of income? In other words, what conditions of *exchange* need to be satisfied for the circular flow to be in a 'stationary state' equilibrium?[2] In *KII* Marx analyses the circulation process, predicated on the process of production analysed in *KI*, to study those equilibrium *exchange* conditions. It is only in *KIII* that he discusses production *and* circulation in a complete model. So before I turn to the transformation problem, let me outline his model of simple reproduction.

The analysis is of a developed capitalist economy, i.e. an economy where money plays a crucial role. The capitalist begins with an amount of money capital with which he buys labour power and raw material. Production takes place, commodities are produced and then sold on the market. Schematically, this is shown below:

$$M \rightarrow \hat{C}(C) \left\langle \begin{array}{l} LP \\ \\ MP \end{array} \right\} \ldots PC \ldots \hat{C}'(C) \rightarrow M'$$

where M is the initial money capital advanced to buy labour power (LP) and raw materials ('material products', MP). This is, in effect, productive (PC). Production takes place (represented by dots) and new commodities $\hat{C}'$ (C) are produced. These are then sold in the market to obtain M' money, ($M' > M$). Note that circulation is interrupted once we reach LP and MP. Production takes place and $\hat{C}'$ is produced. At this stage circulation begins once again. For the purposes of the analysis in the next section, let me formalise the assumptions required for the model of simple reproduction under competitive conditions.

Assumptions

(i) There are three Departments (or Sectors):
Department I produces Capital Goods
Department II produces Consumption Goods
Department III produces Luxury Goods.

It is assumed that within each Department, firms are identical in all respects;

(ii) Capitalists spend all the surplus value on luxury goods and workers spend all their wages on consumption goods. In other words, there is no saving and no net investment in the economy;

(iii) Labour is homogeneous and is the only primary input. The rate of surplus value is uniform over Departments;

(iv) There are no durable capital goods. In other words, the turnover period of capital is one unit of time;

(v) There is no choice of technique for any capitalist in any Department. For each Department, there is one, and only one, technique of production;

(vi) Production is a point-input, point-output process. That is, all inputs are applied at one point in time and all output comes out at some subsequent point of time, within the unit period. (This means we need not worry about the timing of inputs within the period, nor need we worry about the time profile of outputs);

(vii) There are constant returns to scale;

(viii) There are no joint products, i.e. no production process produces two outputs, e.g. wool and mutton;

(ix) The economy is closed (there are no imports or exports) and no technical change takes place;

(x) The organic composition of capital is the same in all Departments.

The model in the value systems can be written as:

$$\begin{array}{ll} & \overbrace{\qquad\qquad\qquad\qquad\qquad}^{\textit{Inputs}} \\ \text{Department I} & c_1(V) + v_1(V) + s_1(V) = w_1(V) \\ \text{Department II} & c_2(V) + v_2(V) + s_2(V) = w_2(V) \\ \text{Department III} & c_3(V) + v_3(V) + s_3(V) = w_3(V) \end{array} \left.\vphantom{\begin{array}{l}a\\a\\a\end{array}}\right\} \textit{Outputs}$$

In Department I, c_1 of constant capital, plus v_1 of variable capital which produces s_1 of surplus value, produces an output of value w_1. Since we have constant returns to scale $\lambda c_1 + \lambda v_1 + \lambda s_1 = \lambda w_1$. We can, therefore, interpret w_1 as being the *total* value produced or, alternatively, the value per unit of output.

Equilibrium requires that the total demand for the constant capital equals the total supply (production) of constant capital, the total demand for consumption goods equals the total supply, and the total demand for luxury goods equals the total supply. In algebraic terms:

$$\begin{aligned} c_1(V) + c_2(V) + c_3(V) &= C(V) = w_1(V) \\ v_1(V) + v_2(V) + v_3(V) &= V(V) = w_2(V) \\ s_1(V) + s_2(V) + s_3(V) &= S(V) = w_3(V) \end{aligned}$$

Note that the above model is stated in the value domain.[3] Of course in a capitalist economy, money intermediates between transactions, so that the prices that result should be such that the supply and demand are equated. The surplus value created goes through the market and is transformed into profits in the price domain. Both the capitalist and the worker see profits emerging from the exchange mechanism and are therefore confused into believing that the *source* of profits is the circulation process. Each Department *produces* a surplus value $s_i(V)$. Under what conditions would the capitalists of each Department (sector) appropriate the amounts of surplus value produced in the respective Department (sector)? What conditions would lead to capitalists in a Department appropriating more (less) than the surplus value created in that Department? In the next section I shall consider the set of (equilibrium) prices that emerge which lead to a redistribution of the surplus value between Departments. This redistribution comes about through the process of *competition* between capitalists that leads to an equalisation of profit rates.

3.3 The Transformation Problem Stated

As is common in discussions of this topic, I shall give numerical illustrations of the transformation problem with a three Departmental economy (as listed in the previous section) even though Marx used a five Departmental illustration in *KIII*. Let me begin with a case where the transformation problem is a non-problem: the case of equal organic compositions of capital.

Table 3.1 is drawn up on the basis of the assumptions set out in the previous section. The first section of the table represents the amounts paid for inputs at 'direct prices'. (See below for a definition.) The units are pounds sterling per unit of time. Capitalists in Department I spend (say) £400 on constant capital and £200 on variable capital per year. The 'cost price' is £600 per year. In *value* terms constant capital is 200 (abstract) labour hours per year, the value of labour power is 100 labour hours per year which produces surplus value of 100 labour hours per year. (I am assuming a 100% rate of exploitation, which is uniform across Departments). The total value is 400 labour hours per year. The value rate of profit

$$\pi(V) = \frac{s(V)}{c(V) + v(V)} = \frac{100}{200 + 100} = 33.33\%$$

Following Shaikh (1977) the assumption of exchange at 'direct prices' means that prices are proportional to values. For example, let 1 labour hour produce 1 ounce of gold which is worth £2. Using the factor of proportionality of 2, we can convert the total value $w_1(V)$ produced in Department I as equal to £800. That implies total profits equal to £200 which gives a rate of profit at direct prices as

$$\pi(DP) = \frac{\Pi(DP)}{C(DP) + V(DP)} = \frac{200}{400 + 200} = 33.33\%$$

Note that the value rate of profit equals the rate of profit at direct

Table 3.1 Exchange at Direct Prices (Equal Organic Compositions of Capital)

Dept.	*Constant Capital C(DP)*	*Variable Capital V(DP)*	*Cost Price k(DP)*	*Value of Constant Capital C(V)*	*Value of Labour Power V(V)*	*Surplus Value S(V)*	*Total Value W(V)*	*Value Rate of Profit % π(V)*	*Total Prices at Direct Prices W(DP)*	*Total Profits at Direct Prices Π(DP)*	*Rate of Profit at 'Direct Prices' % π(DP)*
I	400	200	600	200	100	100	400	33.33	800	200	33.33
II	300	150	450	150	75	75	300	33.33	600	150	33.33
III	200	100	300	100	50	50	200	33.33	400	100	33.33
	£900	£450	£1350	450	225	225	900		£1800	£450	

Table 3.2 Exchange at Direct Prices (Unequal Organic Compositions of Capital)

Dept.	*Constant Capital C(DP)*	*Variable Capital V(DP)*	*Cost Price k(DP)*	*Value of Constant Capital C(V)*	*Value of Labour Power V(V)*	*Surplus Value S(V)*	*Total Value W(V)*	*Value Rate of Profit % π(V)*	*Total Prices at DP W(DP)*	*Total Profit at Direct Prices Π(DP)*
I	450	180	630	225	90	60	375	19.05	750	120
II	200	240	440	100	120	80	300	36.36	600	160
III	100	180	280	50	90	60	200	42.85	400	120
	£750	£600	£1350	375	300	200	875		£1750	£400

prices. Also note that the rate of profit is uniform (equal) over different Departments. Thus if commodities exchanged, *in this example*, at direct prices, rates of profit would be equalised and these direct prices would be *equilibrium* prices. There would be no tendency for capitalists to move their capital from one Department to another in search of a higher rate of profit. Hence for this case (*and for this case alone*, as is demonstrated below) prices of production equal direct prices and the value rate of profit equals the price rate of profit. Marx's analysis in terms of values is not just an 'approximation'. However, note that the above table was derived for a special case, namely, of equal organic compositions of capital:

$$q_1(V) = q_2(V) = q_3(V) = 2$$

Note that we also have total prices (total revenues at direct prices) proportional to total values and total profits proportional to total surplus values. Also note that the profits obtained by capitalists in *each* Department are proportional to the surplus value created in their own Department. No redistribution of surplus value between Departments takes place. If we had assumed the factor of proportionality to equal one, we would have total prices equal to total values and total profits equal to total surplus value.

Now let me remove the simplifying assumption that organic compositions of capital are equal, retaining all the other assumptions. In Table 3.2 we have an economy with different organic compositions of capital. We assume as before that the rate of exploitation is uniform across departments. For this illustration, based on Shaikh (1977), the rate of exploitation is assumed to be 66.67%. Also, as before, 1 unit of labour time produces 1 ounce of gold worth £2.

If we now look at the value rate of profit, $\pi(V)$, we find that it differs from Department to Department. Hence circulation (exchange) at direct prices does not give us an equilibrium: capital would flow from Department I and II to Department III. Hence, if rates of exploitation are equal, prices are proportional to values and organic compositions of capital differ, then the value rates of profit (equal to the rates of profits at direct prices) would differ. Since we know that organic compositions of capital would differ, in general, from Department to Department, either prices cannot be proportional to values, or profit rates cannot be equalised.[4] Since competition between capitalists must lead to an equality of profit rates (in the price domain), prices cannot be proportional to values. This is the crux of the transformation problem. In general, prices *cannot* be proportional to values. Marx was clearly aware of this problem and criticised the Classical economists for believing that prices could be proportional to value.

The transformation problem consists of finding a way of equalising the rate of profit in the *price* domain *even though the value rates are different.* In other words, the circulation process must generate a set of (equilibrium) prices that would lead to an equalised price rate of profit, *given* the production of values and surplus values. Production has taken place, commodities are thrown on the market and the resulting prices must be such as to have made the production in different Departments the 'correct' amounts such that profit rates are equalised. In other words, with the equilibrium set of prices, capitalists in attempting to maximise profits, allocate their capital across Departments which justifies the existing allocation.

As shown above, if prices are proportional to values, the rates of profit are not equal. Hence prices must diverge *systematically* from (in proportionality with) values, such that profit rates in the price domain are equalised. This would lead o a reallocation of surplus value from one Department to another: profits in a Department would no longer be proportional to surplus value in that Department.

3.4 Marx's Solution

Marx's solution consists of redistributing surplus value, which is created according to the amount of variable capital, such that we get an equalised profit rate. Thus the prices of the Departments with below average rates of profit must rise (be more than proportional to values) and prices of Departments with above average profit rates must fall until profit rates are equalised. Again note that the actual amounts of production remain unchanged, hence values and surplus values *produced* remain unchanged. All the changes take place in the variables in the *price* domain as a result of the circulation process. As Marx puts it:

> So far as profits are concerned, the various capitalists are just so many stockholders in a stock company in which the shares of profit are uniformly divided per 100, so that profits differ in the case of the individual capitalists only in accordance with the amount of capital invested by each in the aggregate enterprise, i.e., according to his investment in social production as a whole, according to the number of his shares.
>
> (*KIII*, Ch. IX, p. 158)

It is important to note that as a result of the circulation process, the profits obtained by the capitalists of one Department are no longer proportional to the surplus value created in that Department. The origin and nature of profits is 'mystified' by the circulation process.

Let me turn to the numerical example presented in Table 3.3. Marx's solution consists of finding out the average rate of profit *at direct prices* and then adding this average rate to the cost price *C(DP) + V(DP), at direct prices* to obtain the 'total price' of each Department. (Remember total price is the valuation of commodities in the *price* domain.) As a result of this procedure the direction of movement of prices is correct, Department I's total prices increase and Departments II and III have a fall in total prices. This is illustrated in Table 3.3 (based on Shaikh (1977)).

We begin, as before, with production being as described in the value domain in the middle section of the table. The total amount of surplus value created is 200 units of abstract labour time which converted at direct prices equals £600. The total capital advanced, at *direct prices*, is £1350. Hence $\pi(DP) = 400/1350 = 29.63\%$. This average rate of profit at direct prices is applied to the cost price in each Department to give the profits of that Department. Thus, Department I has a cost price of £630, which obtains a profit of 29.63% of £630 (which is £186.67). The total output is then worth, in the price domain

£630 + £186.67 = £816.67

A similar application of the average profit rate to other Departments gives the total price of that Department. In algebraic terms:

$$\pi(DP) = \frac{\Sigma\, s_i(DP)}{\Sigma[c_i(DP) + v_i(DP)]} = \frac{S(DP)}{C(DP) + V(DP)}$$

$$c_i(DP) + v_i(DP) + \pi(DP)\,[c_i(DP) + v_i(DP)] = w_i(P)$$

where $w_i(P)$ are the total prices, or 'prices of production', given our assumption of constant returns to scale.

Marx has 'transformed' surplus value into profits and transformed values, $w_i(V)$, into prices, $w_i(P)$. Note that in this transformation, total prices are proportional to total values and total profits are proportional to total surplus value. If instead of using 1 labour unit equals £2 we had normalised our measure by setting 1 labour unit equals £1, we would have got Marx's result that total prices equal total values and total profits equal total surplus value. (In this case, direct prices would be equal to values expressed in pounds sterling.)

3.5 Problems with Marx's Solution

(i) Marx converts only the right-hand side terms (the outputs) into the price domain, but leaves the left-hand side terms (the inputs) unchanged. As shown in the previous section, c and v are

Table 3.3 Marx's Solution

Dept.	*C(DP)*	*V(DP)*	*k(DP)*	*C(V)*	*V(V)*	*S(V)*	*W(V)*	*W(P)*	*Π (P)*	*π (DP)* %
I	450	180	630	225	90	60	375	816.67	186.67	29.63
II	200	240	440	100	120	80	300	570.37	130.37	29.63
III	100	180	280	50	90	60	200	362.96	82.96	29.63
	£750	£600	£1350	375	300	200	875	£1750.00	£400.00	

evaluated at direct prices (i.e. they are *not* transformed into prices of production). The average rate of profit is then applied to the cost price ($c + v$), in terms of direct prices. Consistency requires that the inputs must also be transformed into prices of production. Marx was aware of this problem (see *KIII*, Ch IX, p. 158, 161, 164—5) but did not provide a complete and correct solution. See below for a possible resolution of the problem by Shaikh (1977) and Morishima (1973) who use an iterative method to obtain a 'correct solution'.

(ii) Except by accident, this solution will not satisfy the equilibrium conditions of simple reproduction.

(iii) Marx defines the average profit rate in terms of direct prices (or values), but then shows that prices diverge systematically from values, which implies that the rate of profit in terms of 'prices of production' cannot equal the value rate of profit. This is an inconsistency that Steedman (1977) has emphasised.

(iv) It is worth noting that the transformation is purely an analytical construct: it is not describing a dynamic adjustment process.

(v) Note the restrictive assumptions made about no joint products and no choice of technique. See below, Section 3.7.

3.6 Bortkiewicz's Solution[5]

In an early paper criticising Marx, Bortkiewicz (1907) proposed a consistent solution to the transformation problem for the set of assumptions listed in Section 3.2, except that organic compositions of capital differ. He suggests a solution where both the outputs *and inputs* are transformed into the price domain and satisfies the equilibrium condition of simple reproduction. (Essentially this method can be extended to allow for 'steady state' growth as well.)

Rewriting the set of equations of Section 3.2 (and for brevity dropping the parentheses) by transforming them by their respective prices of production (p_i) and imposing the equilibrium conditions we get:

Dept I $p_1c_1 + p_2v_1 + \pi(P)\,(p_1c_1 + p_2v_1) = p_1(c_1 + c_2 + c_3)$

Dept II $p_1c_2 + p_2v_2 + \pi(P)\,(p_1c_2 + p_2v_2) = p_2(v_1 + v_2 + v_3)$

Dept III $p_1c_3 + p_2v_3 + \pi(P)\,(p_1c_3 + p_2v_3) = p_3(s_1 + s_2 + s_3)$

Here we have three equations and four unknowns (p_1, p_2, p_3 and $\pi(P)$) so we cannot derive a unique solution. To find a solution we could add a fourth equation, total prices equal total values *or* total surplus values equal total profits. However, Bortkiewicz suggests we use Department III as the numeraire Department, i.e. set $p_3 \equiv 1$. Thus we now have three unknowns and three equations. (Note we have assumed a uniform price rate of profit, $\pi(P)$, in all Departments. This is because of our competitive assumptions.) Does there exist a solution to this set of equations? We can find a solution to this system of equations which gives positive prices and profit rate if the organic composition of capital in Department I exceeds that in Department II ($q_1 > q_2$). These prices will diverge systematically from values. However, in general, with this method total prices will not equal total values, and total profits will not equal total surplus value. Only in the special case that the organic composition of capital in Department III equals the *average* organic composition of capital of the economy ($q_3 = \bar{q}$) would we get total values equal to total prices and total surplus value equal to total profits. If $p_3 = 1$ and $q_3 \neq \bar{q}$, then total surplus values equal total profits, but total value is not equal to total prices. In general, the rate of profit in the price system will differ from the value rate of profit, $\pi(P) \neq \pi(V)$. If $p_3 \neq 1$, then total surplus value is not equal to total profits. It is also worth noting that in this economy the output of Department III is not an input into *any* Department's output. The price rate of profit resulting from this solution is therefore not, surprisingly, independent of the organic composition of capital and variable capital in Department III.

To illustrate Bortkiewicz's solution, let us look at a numerical table derived using as the 'fourth equation' that total prices equal total values, or to be precise, total prices equal total values *at direct prices*.

Note in Table 3.4 that the equilibrium (equalised) price rate of profit is different from the value rate of profit in Marx's solution. This method also transforms inputs into the price domain.

In an ingenious extension of Marx's transformation solution, Morishima (1973) and Shaikh (1977) provide an iterative solution that gives a consistent solution. If we begin with Marx's solution as a *first* step and then adjust the *input* prices according to the results of the first stage, we get a new set of prices and profit rate and continue this iterative process. The resulting configuration gives the *same* rate of profit, and the same set of prices as the Bortkiewicz solution for the normalisation given in the numerical example above. In this iterative solution, total prices are equal to total direct prices (or proportional to total values). The important point to note about this iterative procedure is that it extends Marx's method, using his insights that the transformation is a redistribution of surplus values in the process of *circulation*.

Table 3.4 Bortkiewicz's Solution

Dept	*C(DP)*	*V(DP)*	*k(DP)*	*C(P)*	*V(P)*	*k(P)*	*C(V)*	*V(V)*	*S(V)*	*W(V)*	*W(P)*	*π(P)*	*π(P)* %
I	450	180	630	504	168	672	225	90	60	375	840	168	25
II	200	240	440	224	224	448	100	120	80	300	560	112	25
III	100	180	280	112	168	280	50	90	60	200	350	70	25
	£750	£600	£1350	£840	£560	£1400	375	300	200	875	£1750	£350	

3.7 Joint Production and Choice of Technique

So far I have assumed the absence of joint productions and choice of techniques. In criticism of Marx's value analysis, Morishima (1973) and Steedman (1977) have emphasised the importance of joint production when we treat *durable* capital goods. In a von Neumann model, a production process produces an output *plus* a machine which is one period older. Even if we ignore joint production of the 'wool and mutton' type, the existence of durable capital goods is much too prevalent to ignore. Using extensions of the Bortkiewicz method, e.g. Seton (1957) and Morishima (1973), we get non-uniqueness of the equilibrium price set. Similarly, if capitalists in a Department could choose from different techniques (processes) or use some combination of two or more processes, then values would not be uniquely determined, if we continue with the definition of value as given earlier. Although these problems are important, I simply refer the reader to the rather more mathematical literature contained in Steedman (1977), Morishima (1973) and Desai (1979). It is interesting to see, however, that Morishima and Catephores (1978) show that if we employ linear programming methods using inequalities, we can derive a consistent set of prices from values. For their solution, total prices equal total values and total profits equal total surplus values, the two conditions Marx obtains. However, they have to define value as the *minimum* amount of labour embodied in a commodity. Using an objective function to minimise labour embodied, they overcome the problems of non-uniqueness mentioned above. In passing it is worth stating that Marx almost always defines value in terms of socially necessary labour embodied under 'average' conditions. Morishima and Catephores, however, do find some textual support for their interpretation.[6] Again, it is not clear why capitalists would want to minimise labour values rather than minimise costs in the price domain. This is not to deny the importance of Morishima and Catephores' contribution in extending Marx's analysis to make it consistent under more general assumptions about the production process.

3.8 Neo-Ricardian Critique

The neo-Ricardian critique of Marx's value theory (inspired by Sraffa) as typified by Steedman (1977), consists of the following points:

(i) Marx does not convert inputs into the price domain;
(ii) Marx uses a *value* rate of profit which is *different* from the price

rate of profit. Capitalists are only concerned with the price rate of profit;

(iii) Marx ignores problems associated with joint production, choice of techniques and dated labour-inputs. The treatment of heterogeneous labour is inadequate;

(iv) Most important of all is the criticism that value theory, even if it could overcome the above problems, is *unnecessary* or redundant. Value theory is an unnccessary detour. *All* (so they argue) of Marx's analysis can be carried out *without* the LTV which is a 'major fetter' on the development of a 'materialist account of capitalist societies' (Steedman (1977), p. 207).

I have already discussed the first three points, and I shall outline Steedman's argument about the 'redundancy' of the LTV.

Steedman argues that if we begin, in the commodity domain, with known technical production coefficients, and a given real wage in terms of a *commodity* bundle, we can determine the rate of profit and equilibrium prices *without going into the value analysis*. He also argues that it can be shown that surplus labour is necessary and sufficient for positive profits *without* using value analysis. Steedman's book is a model of lucidity and makes several important and provocative statements. However, as I shall argue in the next section, it is very un-Marxist! (It is an extremely difficult book to attack, since he pre-empts criticisms by taking 'composite allegations' which he attempts to refute.)

3.9 An Assessment

In the previous sections we have seen that Marx's transformation method is incorrect and that a formally 'correct' method can be used subject to certain restrictive assumptions. Alternatively, following Morishima and Catephores, we can extend Marx's analysis to allow for very general production assumptions as long as we re-define the concept of value in terms of minimum labour embodied. Given that an alternative method exists that transforms from the commodity domain to the price domain, without going through the value analysis, should we jettison the LTV as Steedman *et al*. recommend? Before we can answer this question, let us look at the role of the LTV in Marx's analysis of a capitalist economy.

To reiterate, Marx's analysis in *KI* is of the production process predicated on circulation, but *abstracting* from circulation. In *KII* he analyses the process of circulation predicated on production having taken place. In *KIII* he combines the analysis of production and circulation when there is competition between different capitals. To evaluate the role of the LTV it is important to remember that Marx considers it central for descriptive, predictive and normative purposes.

The most important role that the LTV plays in Marx's writings is to expose the conflict between classes: between capitalists and workers. Society develops as a result of dialectical contradictions and the LTV helps to select and focus on those descriptive aspects that highlight social relationships. As opposed to the neo-Classical economists, whose main emphasis is on prices and neo-Ricardians who begin their analysis with technological relationships, Marx's analysis begins with a study of human relationships. He, therefore, criticises vulgar economists for their fetishism of commodities. Similarly, in studying the nature and origin of profits, Marx was using the LTV as a descriptive theory. Discussions of exploitation are descriptive, even though they obviously have normative overtones. He stressed the fact that profits were not due to the private ownership of the means of production, but due to the existence of surplus labour or surplus value. The importance of the LTV in exposing the 'reality' beneath the 'appearances' is often suggested by Marx. For example, in discussing the transformation problem, he refers to the 'mystification' of surplus value:

> Disguised as profit, surplus-value actually denies its origins, loses its character, and becomes unrecognisable.
>
> (*KIII*, Ch. IX, p. 167)

> *But this is a process which occurs behind his back, one he does not see, nor understand, and which indeed does not interest him.* The actual difference of magnitude between profit and surplus-value — not merely between the rate of profit and the rate of surplus-value — in the various spheres of production now *completely conceals the true nature and origin of profit not only from the capitalist, who has a special interest in deceiving himself on this score, but also from the labourer.* The transformation of values into prices of production serves to obscure the basis for determining value itself.
>
> (*KIII*, Ch. IX, p. 168, emphasis added)

The importance of social compulsion in the extraction of surplus labour is an important aspect that Marx chides Ricardo for ignoring,

> For this [surplus labour] to occur, the labourer must first be *compelled* to work in excess of the [necessary] time, and this compulsion is exerted by capital. This is missing in Ricardo's work, and therefore also the whole struggle over the regulation of the normal working day.
>
> (*TSV II*, p. 406, square brackets added)

For analyses of social relationships and for the analysis of concepts like alienation, the LTV is crucial. Similarly, the LTV helps to explain the importance of the dual nature of labour, its use value being different from its exchange value. (See letter to Engels, 24, August 1867 in *SC*.)

The LTV provides Marx with a method of aggregation to study macroeconomic relationships; see Morishima (1973). It also provides Marx with a predictive theory about prices of production which, it is true, he made mistakes in deriving. This derivation of prices of production for Marx is *not* the most important aspect of the LTV.

Finally, what of the critique, e.g. Robinson (1966) that values are non-observable, a metaphysical concept? Capitalists act and react to prices, not values. Sen (1978) has an interesting discussion refuting this view. As discussed above, the LTV has descriptive and predictive content. It is worth remarking that as regards the neo-Ricardian alternative where prices of production are derived, that these prices are also non-observable. Capitalists react to variables at *market* prices, or to non-observable *expected* prices. Unless they have 'rational expectations' and their expected prices are the long-run equilibrium prices, prices of production and rates of profit at prices of production are also not observed by capitalists. Thus we have to choose between two sets of abstractions: one that uses value analysis and one that does not.

It is important to remember Kuhn's (1970) concept of a paradigm which suggests that Marx's paradigm using the LTV focuses our interest, poses questions, suggests empirical studies where the major interest is on *social* relationships in an economy, and *not* on relative prices. It is not surprising that non-Marxist economists rarely concern themselves with questions of exploitation, alienation, or the labour process. We, therefore, reject Steedman's suggestion to jettison the LTV.

3.10 Summary

In this Chapter, I discussed the problem of transforming surplus value into profits, and values into prices when organic compositions of capital are unequal. After discussing Marx's solution and its limitations, I discussed alternative solutions. Neo-Ricardian criticisms were outlined and the role of the LTV in Marx's analysis was assessed. The crucial role played by the LTV in analysing a capitalist economy was stressed. It is important to remind the reader that prices of production that were determined by the LTV are long-run equilibrium prices. In this explanation demand factors are ignored because of the assumption of constant returns to scale (horizontal supply curves). Market prices (short-run) are explained in terms of conventional supply and demand factors. It is also important to note that, in aggregate, it is assumed that there are no problems of effective demand in the Keynesian sense (or what Marx calls realisation problems).

Notes to Chapter 3

1. See *KI*, Ch. V, p. 166, fn. 1.
2. This is one of the earliest models of general equilibrium following the lines of Quesnay's *Tableau Economique*.
3. In fact, given our assumption of equal organic compositions of capitals, prices are proportional to values and the formal analysis is unchanged. However, if we relax this assumption, the transformation problem rears its ugly head! See the next section.
4. Note that $\pi_i(V) = [s_i'(V)]/[q_i(V) + 1]$. Hence, with $s_i' = s_j'$, $q_i \neq q_j$ implies $\pi_i \neq \pi_j$. Alternatively, $\pi_i = \pi_j$ if and only if $q_i = q_j$. I am, of course, ignoring the degenerate case where $s_i' = 0$. (All variables defined in the value domain). With exchange at direct prices the value and price rates of profit are the same.
5. See Sweezy (1942), Meek (1973) and Desai (1979).
6. See *Poverty of Philosophy* in *CW*, Vol. 6, p. 136.

Further Reading for Chapter 3

1. *KIII* Chs IX, X, L
2. *KII* Ch. XX
3. Sweezy (1942) Ch. 7. (This gives an excellent account of the nature of the transformation problem and Bortkiewicz's solution)
* 4. Desai (1979) Chs 8–13. (This is a very good mathematical account of the transformation problem)
* 5. Morishima (1973) Chs 7, 8, 12, 14. (This provides a clear mathematical account of Marx's economics in a von Neumann setting)
* 6. Morishima & Catephores (1978) Chs 2, 6, 7
7. Steedman (1977) (especially) Chs 1,2
8. Fine & Harris (1979) Ch. 2. (This gives a summary and evaluation of the debate amongst Marxists on this topic)
9. Meek (1973) Introduction
10. Baumol (1974)
11. Shaikh (1977) (This gives a very readable and 'correct' interpretation of the nature of the transformation problem)
12. Himmelweit & Mohun (1975)
*13. Samuelson (1971) (This is an anti-Marxist critique of Marx)
14. Blaug (1980) (This is a provocative critique of Marx's economics)

Note *Advanced mathematical reading

. . . but while the miser is merely a capitalist gone mad, the capitalist is a rational miser.

(*KI*, Ch. IV, p. 153)

4 Capital Accumulation

4.1 Introduction

As I have stressed before, Marx is interested in analysing a capitalist economy in motion. A central determinant of the laws of motion of a capitalist economy is the nature and progress of capital accumulation. In studying the determinants of capital accumulation, I shall distinguish between the individual capitalist and the capitalist class as a whole. I shall also distinguish between determinants of short- and long-run capital accumulation. It is a curious feature of Marxist economics that much controversy has raged over the transformation problem, but relatively little discussion has taken place about capital accumulation (except about concentration). Competitive forces within a capitalist economy lead to capital accumulation which brings in its wake technological change. Although Marx discusses the effects of changes in the rate of profit and/or changes in the wage rate on capital accumulation in the *short-run*, long-run capital accumulation is determined by what are broadly sociological forces. The long-run trend of accumulation, he argues, is increasing, although there are cyclical variations around the trend.

4.2 Objectives of Capitalists

As discussed in Chapter 2, the amount of surplus value created depends on the value of labour power, the length of the working day and the intensity of exploitation. The amount of profit (in the price domain) realised by an individual capitalist, and by the capitalist class as a whole, depends on the competitive process that works through the sphere of circulation (exchange). Capitalists then have to decide how to allocate the profits between:

(a) capitalist consumption; and
(b) accumulation, which is subdivided into:
  (i) additions to constant capital
  (ii) additions to variable capital.

Marx refers to the division between revenue (consumption) and accumulation as a 'deliberate act' (*KI*, Ch. XXIV, p. 591). Note that by accumulation, Marx means spending on constant capital (*which includes raw materials*) and spending on variable capital.

Capitalists in Marx's model are good profit maximising agents, not unlike those in bourgeois economics. They are continually striving to minimise costs and maximise profits by increasing the exploitation of labour and innovating by introducing new and better machinery. To quote Marx, 'the restless never-ending process of profit making alone is what he aims at . . .' (*KI*, Ch. IV, p. 152) (see Section 1.5).

As discussed in the previous chapter, Marx identifies *total* profits with *total* surplus values, even though for an individual capitalist profits are not equal to surplus value created in his enterprise. Note that a large part of the discussion on accumulation is in *KI*, where Marx assumes equal organic compositions of capital and hence prices equal values. This discussion is at a higher level of abstraction. In *KII* Marx's discussion of accumulation is secondary to his concern with studying the process of circulation. In *KIII* Marx's discussion of accumulation should be in the price domain, but he often slips into identifying surplus values with profits for an individual capitalist (as well as for the capitalist class as a whole). Given a constant rate of exploitation, a capitalist can increase the surplus value created by increasing *variable* capital, i.e. employing more labour power. What is it that gives the capitalist an incentive to increase his *constant* capital? If there are fixed coefficients in production, then a capitalist must expand constant capital proportionately with variable capital, i.e. retain a constant organic composition of capital. This, of course, assumes there is no technological change. What is it that *limits* this process of expansion for an *individual* capitalist? In neo-Classical theories of investment (in fixed capital), the existence of a strictly concave production function (diminishing returns to scale) sets a finite limit to the size of the firm. In neo-Classical investment theories, see Junankar (1972), a perfect financial capital market allows the firm to maximise utility in two stages: first maximise profits and then distribute those profits (borrowing and lending where necessary) over time to maximise utility. There is no conflict in this case between consumption and investment.

For Marx, capital accumulation (*additional* expenditure on constant capital *including* raw materials and variable capital) is constrained by the capitalist's realised profits, how much he wishes to consume and what he can raise by borrowing. The development of joint stock companies increased the ability of larger, successful companies to raise increasing amounts of money capital. Smaller capitalists do *not* have equal access to the credit market. Let me first turn to the choice between consumption and accumulation. As a capitalist gets richer, he wants to consume more and accumulate less:

> But along with this growth, there is at the same time developed in his breast, a Faustian conflict between the passion of accumulation, and the desire for enjoyment.
>
> (*KI*, Ch. XXIV, p. 594)

Marx does not really explain how this conflict is resolved, nor whether there is an *increasing* marginal propensity to consume with greater wealth or income. For purposes of his analysis he *assumes*, in effect, a constant marginal propensity to consume (save). (See *KI*, Ch. XXIV, p. 599.)

In addition to the capitalist's desire to maximise profits, he is interested in increasing control (or acquiring power) over workers. This is a sociological objective of the capitalist, not unlike that discussed by some economists when discussing managerial theories of the firm; see for example Baumol (1959) and Marris (1964). In Marx's words:

> To accumulate, is to conquer the world of social wealth, to increase the mass of human beings exploited by him, and thus to extend both the direct and the indirect sway of the capitalist.
>
> (*KI*, Ch. XXIV, p. 592)

Given a marginal propensity to consume out of surplus value, does the capitalist accumulate all of the remaining surplus value? If he does, then there should be no effective demand (realisation) problems: Say's law would hold. However, Marx bitterly attacks Say's law in various places, so perhaps the two positions can be rationalised as follows. In analysing the *short run* there are times when the capitalist does not automatically invest all the surplus value left after consumption, and this causes realisation problems. However, in analysing *long-run* situations we ignore short-run fluctuations and consider the *trend* behaviour of capitalists who invest all their surplus value, after allowing for capitalist consumption.

There is a 'sociological imperative' to accumulate. The function of a capitalist in a capitalist economy is to accumulate.

> Accumulate, accumulate! That is Moses and the prophets! . . . Accumulation for accumulation's sake, production for production's sake . . .
> (*KI*, Ch. XXIV, p. 595)

The capitalist system drives the capitalist to accumulate. *Competition* forces the capitalist to accumulate to survive. The law that governs life in a capitalist jungle is the law of 'survival of the fittest'.

> Only as personified capital is the capitalist respectable. As such he shares with the miser the passion for wealth as wealth. But that which in the miser is a mere idiosyncrasy, is, in the capitalist, the effect of the social mechanism, of which he is but one of the wheels. Moreover, the development of capitalist production makes it constantly necessary to keep increasing the amount of the capital laid out in a given industrial undertaking, and competition makes the immanent laws of capitalist production to be felt by each individual capitalist, as external coercive laws. It compels him to keep constantly extending his capital, in order to preserve it, but extend it he cannot, except by means of progressive accumulation.
> (*KI*, Ch. XXIV, p. 592)

To summarise, the capitalist's objective is to maximise profits, increase his power over workers, and to accumulate to survive in a competitive world.

4.3 Accumulation and the Rate of Profit

In this section I shall discuss the extent to which the rate of profit governs the rate of accumulation. In Chapter 6 I shall study the impact of accumulation on the rate of profit and discuss Marx's 'law of the tendency of the rate of profit to fall'. As discussed in the previous section, one of the main objectives of the capitalist is to increase his profits. Assuming for the time being no technological change, a capitalist can increase his surplus value by employing more labour power, or by increasing the rate of exploitation of the existing workers. The capitalist has to expand his constant capital to maintain a constant organic composition of capital. Thus accumulation would be allocated between constant and variable capital in the same ratio as the existing organic composition of capital. Whether the increase in surplus value means the capitalist increases his *profits* depends on what happens in the process of circulation. As long as other capitalists do not follow the expansion of this capitalist we are studying, and other things remain equal (*ceteris paribus*), prices will remain unchanged so that profits (in the price domain) must increase. It is, therefore, perfectly rational for each individual capitalist to believe that increasing employment and/or the rate of exploitation would increase his profits. However, if all capitalists in this sector (Department) expand production, it is likely to affect the (equilibrium) prices of production and hence the capitalists of that sector may not have increased their profits. What would happen if all capitalists in the economy were to expand employment and/or the rate of exploitation? Total surplus value would increase. For the special case where the organic composition of capital in the 'luxury goods' Department equals the average composition of capital, total surplus values are equal (proportional) to total profits. Hence, total profits in this case would rise. Again, if all Departments were expanding at a uniform rate (steady-state growth) relative prices would remain unchanged and hence total profits would increase with total surplus values.

Now let me turn to the relation between accumulation and the rate of profit. Let me *assume* that there is a tendency for the rate of profit to fall (see Chapter 6). Around this downward trend assume a cyclical path in the profit rate. Does the capitalist's rate of accumulation respond to the rate of profit in the price domain? Specifically, can we postulate a function

$$A(P) = A[\pi(P)], \qquad A' < 0$$

where A denotes accumulation, π the rate of profit in the price domain and A' the derivative with respect to π. It is possible to argue that in Marx's model, short-run fluctuations in accumulation respond negatively to fluctuations in the profit rate in terms of market prices. Capitalists accumulate in order to compensate for the (assumed) downward trend in the rate of profit. When the rate of profit falls below some 'normal' level, capitalists increase accumulation and introduce innovations. To quote Marx:

> Improvements, inventions, greater economy in the means of production, etc. are introduced not at times when prices rise above their average level but when they fall below it, i.e. when profit falls below its normal rate.
> (*TSV* II, Ch. VIII, pp. 26–7)

In the long run, however, the rate of profit depends on the rate of accumulation and not *vice versa*.

$$\pi(P) = f[A(P)] \qquad f' < 0$$

We shall discuss this negative relation in Chapter 6 on the Falling Rate of Profit.

Marx seems to argue that, in the short run, spurts of accumulation take place, substituting capital for labour when the wage rate increases. But in the long run wages are dependent on accumulation:

> To put it mathematically: the rate of accumulation is the independent, not the dependent, variable; the rate of wages, the dependent, not the independent variable.
>
> (*KI*, Ch. XXV, p. 620)

Let me illustrate the relation between the rate of profit and accumulation in Diagram 4.1.

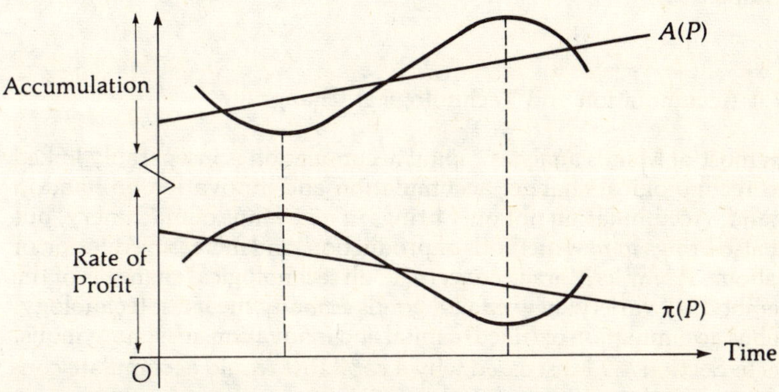

Diagram 4.1 *Accumulation and the Rate of Profit*

The straight lines are the trends of accumulation, $A(P)$ and the rate of profit in the price domain, $\pi(P)$. For the long run *trend* we consider the rate of profit as the dependent variable and the rate of accumulation as the independent variable. However, for cyclical fluctuations, the wavy lines, accumulation falls as the rate of profit rises and rises as the rate of profit falls.

Let me end this section by turning to a possible interpretation of the determinants of accumulation. Since accumulation, in fixed capital, is going to bring in profits over the future, the capitalist must be concerned about expected future sales. For accumulation to continue at a constant rate, expected future sales must *grow* at a constant rate. It is possible to find some quotations in *TSV* to justify an 'accelerator theory' of accumulation which ante-dates, for example, J.M. Clark or Aftalion.

In discussing Ricardo's theory of accumulation, Marx appears to have an accelerator theory:

> For *the production of coal and yarn* and of all other spheres of production which produce only the conditions or earlier phases of a product to be completed in another sphere, is governed not by the immediate demand but by the *degree, measure, proportion* in which these are expanding.
> (*TSV* II, Ch. XVII, p. 531)

Given that in the formal models of reproduction (and in the transformation problem) he assumes fixed coefficients in production, it is easy to derive an accelerator model of accumulation.[1] In recent years accelerator models have been employed to discuss cyclical behaviour. Marx comes near to proposing an accelerator theory of accumulation in his discussion of crises. I shall return to this in Chapter 9.

4.4 Accumulation and Technological Change

In most of Marx's analysis capital accumulation is inseparably linked to technological change: accumulation and innovation go hand in hand. Accumulation not only brings in *new* kinds of machinery, but it also brings in new methods of production, and increasing division of labour. As far as Marx is concerned, all technological change is of the 'embodied' variety: new capital goods embody the latest technology. Thus accumulation of (fixed) capital and innovation are synonymous.

In Section 4.2 I discussed why a capitalist would accumulate constant capital, even though it did not create surplus value. Assuming no technological change, the only justification was to maintain a constant organic composition of capital. The real reason for a capitalist, however, to accumulate constant capital is to introduce *new* technology. It is important to distinguish between the motives of an *individual* capitalist and the capitalist class as a whole. An individual capitalist will attempt to increase productivity by substituting constant capital for labour power. Thus he produces the commodity with smaller amounts of labour embodied than his competitors. Since the *value* of a commodity is the *social* average, the innovating capitalist can capture an excess surplus value. The output is sold according to its *social* value which is greater than the individual innovator's *value*. Competition now forces other capitalists to adopt the *same* methods of production, thus leading to a lowering of the *social* value of the commodity and hence removing the innovator's 'excess' surplus value. Note that it is a dynamic system with continual change taking place. Capitalists want to increase surplus value, but competition tends to reduce any temporary benefits of an innovation. Although the above argument is stated in the value domain, as in Marx's *KI* (see *KI*, Ch. XI, p. 305 and Ch. XII, pp. 317—19), the same applies in the price domain. If one capitalist innovates and produces at lower cost, he can still sell the commodity at its price of production (or just below it) and hence receive excess profits. Marx states this very clearly in *KIII*:

> No capitalist ever voluntarily introduces a new method of production, no matter how much more productive it may be, and how much it may increase the rate of surplus-value, so long as it reduces the rate of profit. Yet every such new method of production cheapens the commodities. Hence, the capitalist sells them originally above their prices of production, or, perhaps, above their value. He pockets the difference between their costs of production and the market-prices of the same commodities produced at higher costs of production. He can do this, because the average labour-time required socially for the production of these latter commodities is higher than the labour-time required for the new methods of production. His method of production stands above the social average. But competition makes it general and subject to the general law. There follows a fall in the rate of profit — perhaps first in this sphere of production, and eventually it achieves a balance with the rest — which is, therefore, wholly independent of the will of the capitalist.
>
> (*KIII*, Ch. XV, pp. 264—5)

> A capitalist working with improved but not as yet generally adopted methods of production sells below the market-price but above his individual price of production; his rate of profit rises until competition levels it out. During this equalisation period the second requisite, expansion of the invested capital, makes its appearance. According to the degree of his expansion the capitalist will be able to employ a part of his former labourers, actually perhaps all of them, or even more, under the new conditions, and hence to produce the same, or a greater, mass of profit.
>
> (*KIII*, Ch. XII, p. 231)

It is interesting to note the similarities of this analysis of a temporary monopoly profit that gets competed away as other capitalists follow suit. This formed the basis of Schumpeter's (1934) well-known *Theory of Economic Development*.

Let me now turn to the type of innovation. In the main Marx postulated that technological change would be labour saving, which accorded with the historical experience of his time. As I shall discuss in Chapters 5 and 6, Marx uses the concept of labour saving technological change to support his theory of an increasing industrial reserve army and falling rate of profit. However, he devotes several pages of *KIII* (see Ch. V, pp. 79ff.) to discussing capital saving innovations. Capital saving innovations include: (i) savings on wastage of (i.e. economising on) raw materials; (ii) re-cycling of waste; (iii) increasing the exploitation of labour, by an increase in the turnover of capital (i.e. a decrease in the period of production); (iv) increasing (physical) life of capital goods by using better materials in the production of machines and by better maintenance; (v) better transport and communications increasing the turnover of capital; and (vi) increasing returns to scale with *new* capital goods lowering the amount of capital used per unit of output. This is quite a remarkable list of capital saving innovations for his time! All of these innovations increase the rate of profit and capitalists are forever searching for new and more efficient production methods. A contradictory force operating is that technological change makes *existing* machinery obsolescent and lowers the *economic* life of machines and hence raises the value of constant capital used. (See *KIII*, pp. 113–4.)

4.5 Accumulation, Concentration and Centralisation

During the process of accumulation there is increasing division of labour in industrial production. Larger firms accumulate at a faster rate than smaller firms because they have greater amounts of profit. Because of increasing returns to scale, larger capitalists have an advantage over small firms. Because larger firms accumulate more rapidly, they produce at a higher scale of operations and hence produce at lower unit costs than small firms. More importantly than the increasing returns to scale argument is that because large firms accumulate faster, they produce with technologically superior machines. Hence small firms are driven into bankruptcy by technically superior (and larger) firms. Hence increasing accumulation leads to increasing *concentration*, that is increasing monopoly.

However, this would be a slow process if it were not aided by a more powerful force in a capitalist economy. This process Marx calls *centralisation*. As larger capitalists accumulate and grow larger and are more powerful, they take over or merge with smaller capitalists. This process is helped by the credit system and the formation of Joint Stock Companies.

> Centralisation may result from a mere change in the distribution of capitals already existing.
>
> (*KI*, Ch. XXV, p. 627)

> ... a new force comes into play — the credit system which in its first stages furtively creeps in as the humble assistant of accumulation, drawing into the hands of individual or associated capitalists, by invisible threads, the money resources which lie scattered, over the surface of society, in larger or smaller amounts; but it soon becomes a new and terrible weapon in the battle of competition and is finally transformed into an enormous social mechanism for the centralisation of capitals.
>
> (*KI*, Ch. XXV, p. 626)

This is one aspect of Marx's theory of capital accumulation that has (deservedly) received much attention.

4.6 An Assessment

Let me begin by summarising this chapter. Marx analyses the laws of motion of a capitalist economy by looking at the dialectical nature of capital accumulation. Noting the competitive nature of capitalism, each individual capitalist in attempting to increase profits accumulates and introduces technological change. Other capitalists imitate and hence negate the advantage of the innovator. The competitive system continues the process. The dialectical process, however, leads to a negation of the competitive system itself: capital accumulation destroys the competitive system and brings in increasing monopoly.

Let me now turn to evaluating Marx's contribution to this area of economics. In assuming profit maximisation behaviour, Marx is in a dominant tradition in economics, then and now. However, he seems to modify this by allowing for certain sociological objectives. Most importantly, however, he stresses the *competitive* nature of accumulation: this aspect is generally ignored by neo-Classical economists. By emphasising the importance of technological change, for capital accumulation and its embodied nature, he is capturing aspects of the real world which have been, in the main, ignored in the neo-Classical literature. For example, an extremely influential and important paper by Jorgenson (1967) on investment completely ignores these problems. Similarly, theories of investment rarely discuss the proposition that a firm can expand its capital stock not by buying new machines, but *by taking over existing firms*. Thus, although Marx does not provide a rigorous mathematical theory of accumulation, he pinpoints certain important aspects which need to be investigated.

Marx's prediction of increasing concentration is one aspect of his theory of capital accumulation that has received much attention. Most casual observers of the industrial scene would agree that industry is much more concentrated now than (say) a hundred years ago. In an extensive study of British industry, Aaronovitch and Sawyer (1975) argue that the casual observer is correct: industry has become more concentrated. Hannah and Kay (1977) are more circumspect, but agree that concentration has increased, although not continuously. Both works emphasise the importance of mergers and take-overs in this process of increasing concentration. It is a sad comment on much of traditional (bourgeois) economics that this increased concentration and, with it, the increased social and political power, is ignored.

Notes to Chapter 4

1. See Junankar (1972) for an elaboration of accelerator theories.

Further Reading for Chapter 4

1. *KI* Chs IV, XXIV, XXV, XXXII
2. *KIII* Chs V, XII, XV
3. *TSVII* Ch. XVII
4. Aaronovitch and Sawyer (1975)
5. Hannah and Kay (1977)

From each according to his ability, to each according to his needs
(Critique of the Gotha Programme)

5 The Industrial Reserve Army

5.1 Introduction

In this chapter I shall discuss Marx's analysis of the Industrial Reserve Army (IRA)[1] and wages. It is one of the contradictions of capitalism that capital both attracts labour (to create surplus value), but also discards labour in the pursuit of profits. In analysing the IRA and wages, it will be useful to distinguish between short- and long-run movements. It is important to remember that Marx is studying a capitalist society in motion: it is *change* that generates an industrial reserve army. Marx argues that capital accumulation leads to a long run increase in the IRA. Along this upward trend movement it displays cyclical behaviour which follows the trade cycle. Wages follow a counter-cyclical path also with an upward trend. (There are contradictory statements about the trend movements of wages, see below.)

It was an important achievement for Marx to have shown that the capitalist system did not automatically generate full employment as most Classical economists believed (with the notable exceptions of Malthus and Ricardo).[2] The crux of the argument lies in the labour displacing nature of technological change and the cyclical behaviour of the economy. Ricardo had at one time followed the Classical economists but, in the third edition of *Principles*, he recanted and produced the famous chapter *On Machinery*. Although Marx is unsparing in his vituperation for Malthus' *Essay on Population*, he gives him credit for discussing unemployment.

The outline of the remainder of this chapter is as follows: in Section 2 I shall explain Marx's concept of the IRA and the sources from which it originates; in Section 3 I shall discuss the relation between the IRA and wages; in Section 4 I turn to the IRA and 'immiserisation'; and Section 5 concludes with an assessment.

5.2 Industrial Reserve Army: Nature and Sources

The industrial reserve army is a pool of unemployed, or partially unemployed, workers that is continually changing in size and composition. (See *KI*, Ch. XXV, p. 640.) Accumulation of capital affects both the demand *and the supply* of labour. Capital accumulation, Marx assumes, is a labour saving process which generates unemployment. Assume a capitalist introduces a labour saving machine in one industry which makes some workers redundant. These unemployed workers decrease their demand for a particular set of commodities. This leads to a fall in price and decrease in production of those commodities and hence a decrease in employment. The initial effect has been magnified by (negative) multiplier effects (*KI*, Ch. XV, p. 438 ff.). There is a partially offsetting increase in the demand for labour to produce the machines now being employed. This depends on the organic composition of capital in the machine producing sector, as well as the rate of exploitation in that sector. On the whole Marx argues that this process leads to an increase in unemployment. Overall Marx assumes that capital accumulation leads to an increasing organic composition of capital (see *KI*, Ch. XV, pp. 430 & 439).

As mentioned earlier, Marx argues that the IRA has an increasing trend with short-run cyclical movements superimposed on the trend. The factors that generate the IRA in the long run are:

(a) Technological change (i) in agriculture
(ii) in industry
(b) Increased Participation Rate and
(c) Population growth.

(a) (i) *Technological Change in Agriculture.* The growth of capitalism leads to a change from feudal 'primitive' agriculture to capitalist 'modern' (mechanised) agriculture. Agricultural labour is displaced and joins the IRA. Both technological and institutional change give this result.

(ii) *Technological Change in Industry.* Capital accumulation throws workers on to the industrial scrap heap. At the same time small capitalists get bankrupted and are forced to join the IRA. It is important to note that many of these may subsequently get employed, but the continuing nature of technical change adds new workers to the IRA.[3]

(b) *Increased Participation Rate.* Capital accumulation initially brings new workers into capitalist enterprise: women and young children are conscripted into the work force. At the same time, increasing rates of exploitation increase the flows of labour services from any given stock of labour. Finally, due to technical change, the labour supply in 'efficiency' units increases more than proportionately to the increase in numbers of potential workers.

(c) *Population Growth.* New entrants into the labour market join the IRA. Although Marx castigates Malthus for his population theory, he nonetheless argues that in periods of relative prosperity the population growth rate rises and in periods of depression it decreases (*KI*, Ch. XXV, p. 643; *KIII*, Ch. XV, pp. 254–5).

Capitalists, on the one hand, can hire more unskilled workers with the same amount of variable capital (as skilled workers are replaced by unskilled) but, on the other hand, they need to hire fewer workers because they extract more labour power (labour services) because of the existence of the IRA.

> Capital works on both sides at the same time. If its accumulation, on the one hand, increases the demand for labour, it increases on the other, the supply of labourers by the 'setting free' of them, whilst at the same time the pressure of the unemployed compels those that are employed to furnish more labour, and therefore *makes the supply of labour*, to a certain extent, *independent of the supply of labourers.*
>
> (*KI*, Ch. XXV, p. 640, emphasis added.)

Besides the upward trend of the IRA there are cyclical fluctations in the IRA due to the trade cycle (see below).

The IRA consists of floating, latent and stagnant components (*KI*, Ch. XXV, p. 641). The floating component consists of workers who are temporarily laid off by modern industry, and those made redundant who find employment in alternative industries. The latent component consists of agricultural workers who are more-or-less redundant in agriculture, but who have yet to make the move to the industrial sector. The stagnant component consists of those workers with 'extremely irregular employment' (*KI*, Ch. XXV, p. 643). It is not clear whether Marx treats 'paupers' as a separate component of the IRA, or whether it is a subset of the floating component (see *KI*, Ch. XXV, p. 643).

It is worth reiterating that the IRA is a *stock* of workers with continual flows adding to and leaving from it. Capital accumulation is a two edged sword: it both increases the flows to the IRA *and* increases the flows out of the IRA (the new employees). The net effect on the IRA depends on whether the inflows exceed the outflows or *vice versa*. A diagrammatic presentation as shown in Diagram 5.1 may help.

Since industrial activity follows a decennial cycle, the IRA goes down during a boom and increases during a recession. The law that determines the IRA is 'a law of population peculiar to the capitalist mode of production' (*KI*, Ch. XXV, p. 632).

As can be seen from the diagram, the IRA is replenished from the agricultural sector, the industrial sector and from new entrants into the labour force. Over the period that Marx was considering, the agricultural sector was an important source for the IRA and so were the new entrants due to increased participation of women and children in the industrial labour force. At the time of his writing, most of the technological change was of the labour saving type. Thus labour made redundant from industry would only get re-asborbed if aggregate demand and production increased sufficiently to employ labour, even though the organic composition of capital was higher. Alternatively, the labour made redundant in consumption goods industries could be employed in the production of machines. Here Marx makes an important point that, unless the increase in demand for machines continued, the machine goods sector would have to cut back production: that is an accelerator relationship applied. (See *KI*, Ch. XV, p. 439.)

It is clear that Marx's prediction of an increasing IRA has been rejected by historical trends. After a certain stage, the flow of labour from agriculture has slowed down and the participation rate fallen due to factory acts that prohibited capitalists hiring children and women. Compulsory schooling for children had a similar effect. Perhaps most importantly, technological change has not been labour saving in aggregate. This is not to deny the existence of labour saving technological change in particular industries at particular times. For instance, the increasing unemployment in the late seventies and early eighties may partly be the result of the microprocessor (chips) revolution.

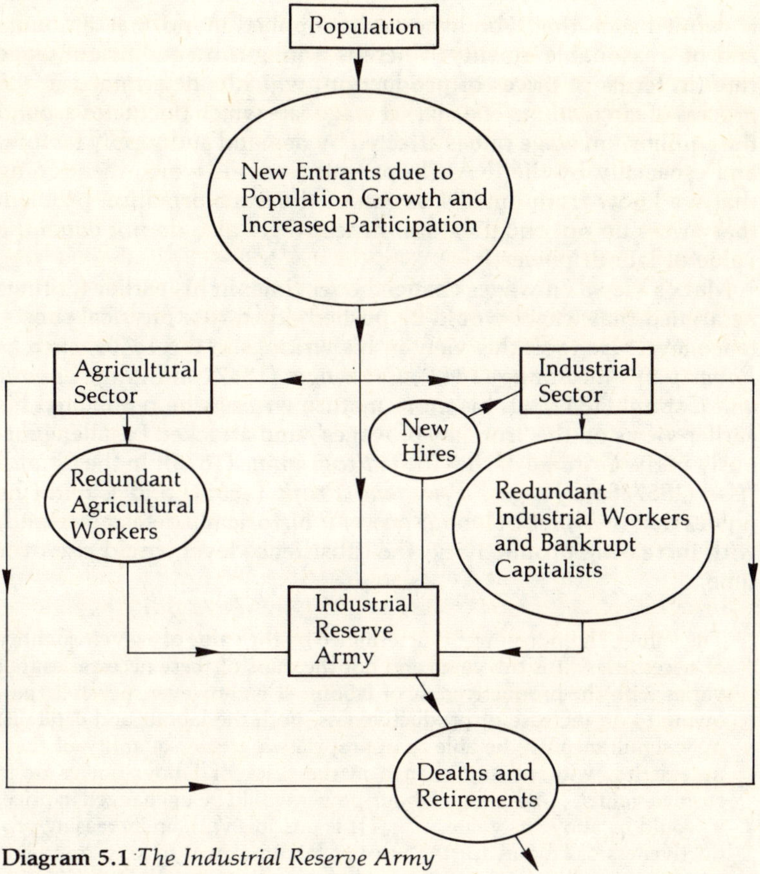

Diagram 5.1 *The Industrial Reserve Army*

5.3 IRA and Wages

In this section I shall discuss the commonly held view that the IRA's role in Marx's model is identical to that of production in Malthus' model, namely to bring wages down to the subsistence level. Let me begin by reminding the reader that the value of labour power is defined by Marx as the value of the commodity bundle necessary to produce and reproduce labour power.[4] It is important to note that the value of labour power is defined *independently* of market conditions, that is independently of the circulation process. In other words, the value of labour power is independent of labour demand, labour supply, or the IRA. To be precise, the value of labour power is defined such that labour power is supplied in 'normal' amounts and of 'reasonable' quality. There is a long-run equilibrium wage rate (in terms of prices of production) which is determined in the process of circulation. The market wage rate which fluctuates around the equilibrium wage rate is affected by demand and supply factors, and especially by the IRA. (In parentheses it is worth mentioning that we know from our discussion of the transformation problem that prices do not equal values, hence wages also do not equal the value of labour power.)

Marx's views on wages changed over time; in his earlier writings he argued that wages would be pushed down to a physical subsistence level. He took this view in his writings in the 1840s, such as *Poverty of Philosophy* (1847), *On Wages* (1847) and *Wage Labour and Capital* (1849). In his more mature writings he repudiated his earlier views on the 'iron law of wages', and attacked Lasalle vigorously in the *Critique of the Gotha Programme* (1875). In the *Grundrisse* (1857/58), *Wages, Price and Profit* (1865), and *Capital* he argues that the value of labour power is historically determined and, with increasing productivity, the subsistence level would rise over time.

> The value of labour-power is determined by the value of a given quantity of necessaries. It is the value and not the mass of these necessaries that varies with the productiveness of labour. It is, however, possible that, owing to an increase of productiveness, both the labour and capitalist may simultaneously be able to appropriate a greater quantity of these necessaries, without any change in the price of labour-power or in surplus-value . . . Although labour-power would be unchanged in price, it would be above its value. . . . [I]t is possible with an increasing productiveness of labour, for the price of labour-power to keep on falling and yet this fall to be accompanied by a constant growth in the mass of the labourer's means of subsistence. But even in such a case, the fall in the value of labour-power would cause a corresponding rise of surplus-value, and thus the abyss between the labourer's position and that of the capitalist would keep widening.
>
> (*KI*, Ch. XVII, p. 523)

It is important to note that Marx clearly envisions an increase in the real wage rate (in terms of the 'mass of necessaries') due to increasing productivity, even though the wage rate in the price system is constant or falling. The value of labour power *falls* because of increasing productivity. As explained in Chapter 2 above, the value of labour power is a long-run concept which is independent of demand and supply. The value of labour power varies across countries and over time. There is a 'moral and historical' element in the value of labour power.[5] The long-run equilibrium wage rate, which is determined by the value of labour power, would rise with increasing productivity. Although there is a *physical* minimum to the value of labour power, the historical and social element is flexible: it is this that increases over time. It is worth stressing that the value of labour power is not *purely* an economic concept determined by economic factors: it is in truly Marxist fashion determined by political, social, historical and economic factors. Hence Marx has no need to use Malthus' law of population to explain the value of labour power.

Given the above discussion, how does one interpret Marx's statement that, 'the rate of accumulation is the independent, not the dependent, variable; the rate of wages, the dependent, not the independent variable' (*KI*, Ch. XXV, p. 620). As I argued in Chapter 4, this should be treated as a long-run argument. It is clear that accumulation leads to increasing productivity and hence the real wage (the mass of necessaries) increases. The long-run wage rate (in the price system) therefore increases with accumulation, although there are other factors that also affect it. One of the socio-political factors that may increase the real wage rate is the unionisation of workers and their increasing power in industrial bargaining. This power is, of course, limited by the IRA. (I shall turn to cyclical fluctuations in the market wage rate after discussing the long-run wage rate). How is it possible for the long-run equilibrium wage rate to increase with an *increasing* long-run IRA? As discussed above, the value of labour power is *not* determined by labour demand and supply; hence, nor is the long-run equilibrium wage rate.

In the Malthusian and Ricardian model, population increases push wages down to a subsistence level and hence allow profits to be made and the economy continues until it reaches the stationary state. In the Marxian model we have argued that there is no such mechanism to keep wages at a subsistence level. What is it that then maintains the equilibrium wage rate at a level that guarantees the existence of surplus value and hence profits? Ignoring the transformation problem for the moment, if the price of a commodity exceeds its value, profit maximising capitalists expand production and price falls until prices equal values. For labour, if wages exceed the value of labour power there is no mechanism for the expansion of labour supply to bring about an equality of wages with value. Sweezy (1942) and Dobb (1973) argue that the IRA provides this mechanism: the IRA pushes down the wages to the minimum subsistence level — the value of labour power. There is, however, a confusion in this argument: wages are in the price system and *not* equal to the value of labour power in the value system.[6] This is clear from our discussion of the transformation problem in Chapter 3. The crucial question is what in Marx's model guarantees the existence of surplus value and hence profits. The answer to this question is at once easy and complex: it is the capitalist system itself that guarantees the existence of surplus value and profits. If the capitalist system does not generate profits it must collapse, since profits are the *raison d'être* of a capitalist.

> If this quantity of unpaid labour supplied by the working-class and accumulated by the capitalist class, increases so rapidly that its conversion into capital requires an extraordinary addition of paid labour, then wages rise, and, all other circumstances remaining equal, the unpaid labour diminishes in proportion. But as soon as this diminution touches the point at which the surplus-labour that nourishes capital is no longer supplied in normal quantity, a reaction sets in: a smaller part of revenue is capitalised, accumulation lags, and the movement in rise in wages receives a check. The rise of wages therefore is confined within limits that not only leave intact the foundations of the capitalist system, but also secure its reproduction on a progressive scale.
>
> (*KI*, Ch. XXV, p. 620)

To repeat, it is not the IRA that guarantees positive surplus value, but it is the nature of the capitalist system itself that does so. If wages are rising too rapidly, accumulation collapses and a crisis follows which contains the increase in wages. (I shall return to a discussion of crises in Chapter 9.)

Let me now turn to the more interesting discussion of fluctuations in market wage rates. As discussed earlier, Marx argues that the value of a commodity and its long-run equilibrium price cannot be explained in terms of supply and demand. However, the fluctuations in market prices (or wages) are explained in terms of (almost orthodox) supply and demand. The cyclical behaviour of the IRA (with the trade cycle) leads to counter-cyclical fluctuations in wages. Thus, when there is a spurt of accumulation, labour demand increases and the IRA decreases: this leads to increased wages. This in turn leads to lower profits, accumulation slows down, the IRA increases and wages decrease.

> Taking them as a whole, the general movements of wages are *exclusively* regulated by the expansion and contraction of the industrial reserve army, and these again correspond to the periodic changes of the industrial cycle. They are, therefore, not determined by the variations of the absolute number of the working population, but by the varying proportions in which the working-class is divided into active and reserve army . . .
>
> (*KI*, Ch. XXV, p. 637, emphasis added)

> The industrial reserve army, during periods of stagnation and average prosperity, weighs down the active labour-army; during the periods of

> over-production and paroxysm, it holds its pretensions in check. Relative surplus population is therefore the pivot upon which the law of demand and supply of labour works. It confines the field of action of this law within the limits absolutely convenient to the activity of exploitation and to the domination of capital.
>
> (*KI*, Ch. XXV, p. 639)

Marx argues that the general movements of wages are determined *exclusively* by the IRA. The context suggests, as does the remainder of the quotation, that he is referring to *cyclical variations* in wages. The IRA varies with the trade cycle and leads to counter-cyclical variation in wages. Accumulation affects *both* the demand and supply of labour (see *KI*, Ch. XXV, p. 640) and fluctuations in accumulation (due to the trade cycle) lead to fluctuations in the IRA and hence in wages. It is in this context he rejects the Malthusian explanation on two counts. First, there is a long lag between an increase in wages and an increase in population of *working age*. Secondly, an increase in the wage rate stimulates the capitalist to introduce labour saving technology and hence increases the IRA. It is clear that Marx is arguing that a high IRA puts a downward pressure on wages, not only because the supply of labour exceeds demand, but also because a high IRA *weakens the bargaining power of trade unions*. Thus wages are not determined in neo-Classical competitive markets, but in quasi-competitive markets with bargaining power influencing wage determination. This bargaining power is limited within the confines that allow the expansion and continuation of the capitalist system: wages must be at least as great as the historically given subsistence level, but cannot be too high, as this would mean low profits and hence a blunted incentive for capitalists.

Diagram 5.2 illustrates the cyclical variation in wages and the IRA.

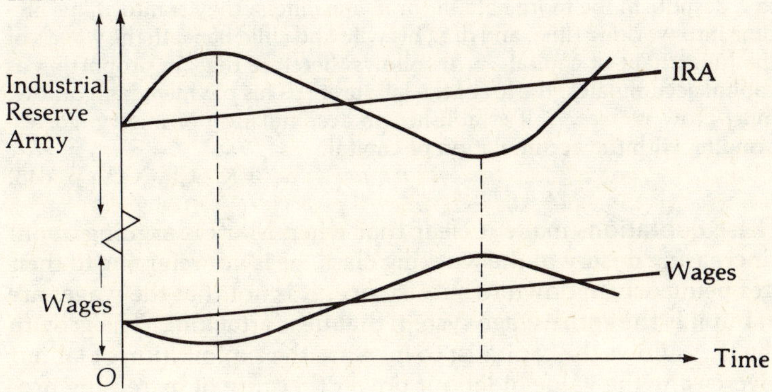

Diagram 5.2 *The Industrial Reserve Army and Wages*

5.4 IRA and Increasing Misery

As discussed above, Marx's concept of a subsistence level allowed for increases in that level over time. Except in some earlier writings, he clearly expected this level to increase. Again, increasing productivity allows the real wage (in terms of the commodity bundle) to increase over time. Although Marx sometimes refers to the wages being driven down to a minimum, it is clear that what he means by increasing misery is the increasing alienation of the working class.

> The greater the social wealth, the functioning of capital, the extent and the energy of its growth, and therefore, also the absolute mass of the proletariat and the productiveness of its labour, the greater is the industrial reserve army . . . But the greater this reserve army in proportion to the active labour-army, the greater is the mass of a consolidated surplus population, whose misery is in inverse proportion to its torment of labour. The more extensive, finally, the lazarus-layers of the working class and the industrial reserve army, the greater is official pauperism. *This is the absolute general law of capitalist accumulation*. Like all other laws it is modified in its working by many circumstances, the analysis of which does not concern us here.
>
> (*KI*, Ch. XXV, p. 644)

> . . . within the capitalist system all methods for raising the social productiveness of labour are brought about at the cost of the individual labourer; all means for the development of production transform themselves into means of domination over, and exploitation of, the producers; they mutilate the labourer into a fragment of a man, destroy every remnant of charm in his work and turn it into a hated toil; they estrange from him the intellectual potentialities of the labour-process in the same proportion as science is incorporated in it as an independent power; they distort the conditions under which he works, subject him during the labour-process to a despotism the more hateful for its meanness; they tranform his lifetime into working time, and drag his wife and child beneath the wheels of the Juggernaut of capital . . . It follows therefore that, in proportion as capital accumulates, the lot of the labourer, be his payment high or low, must grow worse . . . It establishes an accumulation of misery, corresponding with the accumulation of capital.
>
> (*KI*, Ch. XXV, p. 645)

These quotations make it clear that when Marx is arguing about the increasing misery of the working class, he is *not* referring to their wages being driven down to subsistence. It is not that the wages are low, but it is the entire wage system that he is attacking. The growth of the IRA allows the capitalist to increase the exploitation of labour by decreasing the value of labour power (because of increasing productivity), increasing the intensity of labour and weakening the bargaining power of workers. But most important of all, the growth of capitalism leads to increasing alienation.

It is interesting in passing to note that Marx rejects the demand for equal pay:

> The cry for an *equality of wages* rests, therefore, upon a mistake, is an *insane* wish never to be fulfilled . . . Upon the basis of the wages system the value of labouring power is settled like that of every other commodity; and as different kinds of labouring power have different values, or require different quantities of labour for their production, they *must* fetch different prices in the labour market. To clamour for *equal* or *even equitable retribution* on the basis of the wages system is the same as to clamour for *freedom* on the basis of the slavery system.
>
> (*Wages, Prices and Profit, SWI*, p. 426)

5.5 An Assessment

I began this chapter by emphasising the importance of *change* in generating an industrial reserve army. Capital accumulation in a dialectical way produces contradictory results: it increases employment and it increases the IRA. Capital accumulation increases wages, but also increases exploitation..The increase in wages leads to further labour saving capital accumulation and hence an increase in the IRA. Even though real wages increase, the degradation and alienation of workers also increase. An important aspect of the IRA is to provide a reservoir of labour for bursts of expansion. I shall discuss this in Chapter 9 on Crises.

As I have already discussed, history has not been kind to Marx's prediction of an increasing IRA. I suggested that this may have been because the surplus population in agriculture has been more-or-less exhausted and the participation rate of women and children decreased partly due to the strength of the union movement. Most importantly, unlike the mid-nineteenth century, capital accumulation has apparently not been of the labour saving type in aggregate.[7] Several econometric studies suggest that, in aggregate, technological change has been 'neutral'. This is not the place to discuss the theoretical and empirical problems associated with these econometric studies.

At the time of writing, the western capitalist countries are going through a severe recession with unemployment climbing rapidly. The high unemployment is certainly keeping the workers' 'pretensions in check'! Whether this is simply a cyclical down turn or a long-term trend is difficult to forecast.

As regards the value of labour power, in the short run it is an institutionally given datum. Over time it increases due to increasing productivity, but at an unspecified rate. Marx clearly does not have a formalised theory of how the value of labour power changes over time. The long-run equilibrium wage rate is also an institutionally given datum at any point in time. However, it increases over time as the value of labour power increases. The short-run wage rate is determined partly by supply and demand for labour and partly by the relative strengths of the 'combatants' in the bargaining process. Hence there is an 'indeterminacy' of the short-run wage rate. It is interesting to see that Marx very clearly distinguished between nominal and real wage rates, as he did between wage rates in a particular occupation and wage rates in general. Most important of all, he discusses the alienating nature of capitalism. In the *Critique of the Gotha Programme* he discusses the method of payment under a communist society. In the first phase payment would be proportional to the labour provided, but in a higher phase each worker would be paid according to his needs.

Notes to Chapter 5

1. A useful abbreviation, but not to be confused with the Irish nationalist organisation!
2. See Chapter 9 on crises, where the cyclical behaviour of the IRA is discussed in more detail.
3. While travelling in Australia I came across this 'gem' in *The (Melbourne) Age* (26 December 1980):

   > Union leader John Halfpenny says that the claim that technology creates jobs for people it replaces 'is a bit like suggesting that at the time of the invention of the internal combustion engine, all the horses that were going to be displaced by the motor car could have got jobs making the cars'.

4. See Section 2.6 where this is discussed in detail.
5. This is discussed in detail in *Wages, Price and Profit* (1865).
6. I am grateful to Professor Baumol for clarifying this point in a letter to me.
7. Recent trends toward automation, however, suggest increasing labour saving technical change. A report in *The Times* (6 March 1981) talks about robots producing robots in Japan. A spokesman for Hitachi is reported to have said: 'In five years we expect all blue collar workers to disappear from the assembly line. Factories will be manned only by clerical staff and a few maintenance technicians.' Fujitsu Fanuc Ltd. hopes to 'realise an industrialist's ultimate dream in the near future: a factory without any workers at all.' Perhaps Marx's fears about technological unemployment were not unfounded.

Further Reading for Chapter 5

1. *KI* Chs XV, XXIV, XXV
2. *Wages, Price and Profit* (1865) in *SWI*
3. Rowthorn (1980) Ch. 7
4. Steindl (1952) Ch. XIV
5. Sowell (1960)
6. Baumol (1976)
7. Sweezy (1942) Ch. 5
8. Dobb (1973) Ch. 6

The tendency of the rate of profit to fall as society progresses. *This follows from . . .* **the changes in the composition of capital following the development of the social productive forces.** *This is one of the greatest triumphs over the* **pons asinorum** *of all previous economics.*

(Marx to Engels, *SC*, 30 April 1868)

6 The Falling Rate of Profit

6.1 Introduction

In discussing the Law of the Tendency of the Rate of Profit to Fall, Marx believes that he has discovered an important element in the explanation of the 'laws of motion' of a capitalist economy. The law of the falling rate of profit has played an important role in the history of economic thought. Classical economists argued that the law of diminishing returns in agriculture (without technical change) would lead to a falling rate of profit and hence, eventually, to a 'stationary state' with a zero rate of net investment. In contrast, Marx discusses his law of the falling rate of profit in a dynamic context, with technical change leading to *increasing* productivity. Marx argues that increasing capital accumulation leads to an increasing organic composition of capital and hence to a fall in the rate of profit. The falling rate of profit leads capitalists to accumulate and innovate to prevent the fall in the rate of profit. At the same time, it leads to concentration and centralisation.

To understand Marx's analysis it is important to remember Marx's Hegelian background. The Law is developed in Part III of *KIII* where the Chapters are headed:

Ch XIII The Law as Such
Ch XIV Counteracting Influences
Ch XV Exposition of the Internal Contradictions of the Law

Thus the Law is to be understood as two opposing forces that are contradictory: the resolution of the contradictions creates the movement within the system. These counteracting forces are what convert the Law into a 'tendency'. It is important to remember that these counteracting influences are not accidental, but an integral part of the dialectical process.

As this is one of the most controversial aspects of Marx's economics, (that is after the transformation problem), I shall first outline Marx's arguments and then discuss the criticisms. Although Marx discusses this Law in *KIII* after the tranformation problem (at least in the way that Engels put the volume together), the analysis is in value terms, that is, assuming proportionality between values and prices. In my discussion I shall distinguish between the behaviour of an individual capitalist and that of the capitalist class as a whole. I shall also distinguish between cyclical (short-run) movements and long-run trend movements. The analysis will force us to discuss the determinants of accumulation (see Chapter 4) and the nature of technical progress (see Chapters 4 and 5). The plan of this chapter is as follows: Section 2 discusses various definitions and meanings of the Rate of Profit; Sections 3, 4 and 5 outline respectively the Law, its counteracting influences and internal contradictions as stated by Marx; Section 6 discusses criticisms of the Law; Section 7 briefly reviews some evidence; and Section 8 concludes with an assessment.

6.2 On Rates of Profit

As I explained in Chapters 2 and 3, Marx identified total surplus values with total profits. Although this is valid only under certain restrictive assumptions, the exposition and analysis in this chapter will be greatly facilitated by making the necessary assumptions. Nothing of substance is lost in the simplification. It is worth noting that profits for Marx include rents, interest and industrial profits. Thus when Marx refers to a falling rate of profit, it does *not* imply a falling rate of industrial profits: the average rate may fall if the other two components fall, while the rate of industrial profits rises. It is important to keep this in mind when we make comparisons with Classical or neo-Classical writers.

Once the transformation problem has 'reared its ugly head' we have to distinguish the value rate of profit, $\pi(V)$, from the prices of production rate of profit, $\pi(P)$. It will also be useful to distinguish the rate of profit in terms of *market* prices, $\pi(MP)$. The value rate of profit was defined in Chapter 2, Section 12 as:

$$\pi(V) = \frac{S(V)}{C(V) + V(V)}$$

This is Marx's definition of the rate of profit. Notice that the rate of profit is defined for *total* capital advanced by the capitalist. Marx assumes, in effect, that the capitalist *advances* wages to workers, that is, workers are paid wages at the beginning of the period of production. Also note that the rate of profit must be less than the rate of surplus value as long as constant capital is positive.

The prices of production rate of profit is defined as

$$\pi(P) = \frac{\Pi(P)}{C(P) + V(P)}$$

The rate of profit in terms of market prices is defined as

$$\pi(MP) = \frac{\Pi(MP)}{C(MP) + V(MP)}$$

where the parentheses refer to market prices. We know from Chapter 3 that $\pi(V)$ and $\pi(P)$ differ from each other. We also know that market prices differ from long-run equilibrium prices (from prices of production), hence $\pi(MP)$ differs from $\pi(P)$. It is possible to show that $\pi(V)$ and $\pi(P)$ will vary together; see Morishima (1973, p. 64) and Shaikh (1980). However, there is no obvious relation between $\pi(MP)$ and $\pi(P)$, except that the trend of $\pi(MP)$ must be the same as $\pi(P)$. Capitalists do not see $\pi(V)$, nor do they perceive $\pi(P)$: they are unobservable variables. They observe $\pi(MP)$ and, presumably, respond to movements in this *market* variable. The Law of the falling rate of profit is a long-term law and is meant to apply to $\pi(V)$ or $\pi(P)$.

Let me now turn to another complicating factor. As I have argued, constant capital, C, is a measure of the *flow* of capital used up in the process of production. It includes raw materials used up in the process of production, plus the amount of fixed capital (machinery) that gets used up i.e. depreciated. Strictly speaking, the rate of profit is defined for the total capital *stock*, so that unless a unit turnover period of capital is assumed, the rate of profit will differ from the one given above. Marx discusses the problem of different turnover periods in *KII* and mentions it in *KIII*. Engels adds a special Chapter IV to *KIII* to make up for an elaboration that Marx had meant to include, but due to the unfinished nature of the manuscript was never written.

Once we allow for different turnover periods of capital, the definition of the rate of profit is altered to

$$\pi(V) = \frac{S(V)}{\lambda_1 C(V) + \lambda_2 V(V)}$$

where λ_1 and λ_2 are turnover periods for constant and variable capital respectively. A similar correction has to be made for $\pi(P)$ and $\pi(MP)$. Again for simplicity of exposition, we shall assume, as Marx often does, that there is a unit turnover period so that $\lambda_1 = \lambda_2 = 1$.

It is interesting to compare Marx's definition of the rate of profit with neo-Classical (or bourgeois) definitions. In neo-Classical (bourgeois) terms, the concept of profits excludes interest and rent. The rate of profit, as such, is usually not defined or discussed. In some neo-Classical models production is instantaneous, so that the rate of profit, sometimes identified with the marginal product of capital,[1] is defined only for *fixed* capital (which is a subset of Marx's constant capital). In full general equilibrium models of the Arrow-Debreu variety, there is a complete set of perfect markets: there are perfect forward markets so that no capital has to be advanced even if production takes time. In fact, in these models there is no distinction between workers and capitalists: capitalists can hire workers, or workers can hire capital!

Sometimes orthodox economists identify the internal rate of return with the rate of profits. The internal rate of return is that rate at which a stream of net revenues must be discounted to equal the price of the capital good.[2] Again, they are ignoring circulating capital (in Marx's language variable capital plus the raw materials element of constant capital). Accounting definitions of the rate of profit sometimes include the inventories of raw materials and work in progress in the denominator and profits including interest in the numerator. (Precise definitions will be specified in the review of empirical work.)

6.3 The Law Stated

As mentioned in the introduction, Marx discusses the Law of the tendency of the rate of profit to fall in the value domain. It is first stated assuming that the rate of exploitation is constant:

> . . . the gradual growth of constant capital in relation to variable capital must necessarily lead to a *gradual fall of the general rate of profit*, so long as the rate of surplus value, or the intensity of exploitation of labour by capital, remain the same.
>
> (*KIII*, Ch. XIII, p. 212)

As mentioned above, the rate of profit is defined by Marx as

$$\pi(V) = \frac{S(V)}{C(V) + V(V)} = \frac{s'(V)}{q(V) + 1}$$

where $q(V) = C(V)/V(V)$ is the organic composition of capital.

As discussed in previous chapters, he argues that in a capitalist economy there is a tendency for the organic composition of capital to rise because of substitution of labour power by machines and because, in increasing productivity, more raw materials are used up in the unit period of production. Thus if s' is assumed constant and q increases over time, $\pi(V)$ must fall. This is Marx's demonstration of the Law. By assumption he considers an equilibrium rate of profit: due to competitive forces the rate of profit is equalised across all departments.

The demonstration of the Law discussed above is very 'mechanical'. A more subtle demonstration involving economic arguments rests on competitive accumulation. Competitive forces compel capitalists to accumulate and innovate. The leading innovator has a temporary advantage and can sell his output at less than the prevailing equilibrium price. This is because accumulation by the leading innovator lowers his unit costs as well as, Marx believes, labour embodied per unit of output. Competition forces imitation and hence eventually a lowering of the equilibrium output price. Accumulation is usually accompanied by concentration and centralisation. Although there is a fall in the rate of profit, total surplus values and total profits increase. Total surplus value increases because, although the capitalist uses *relatively* more constant capital, he uses *absolutely* more labour power. This does not necessarily mean that more *workers* are employed. A greater amount of labour power may be extracted from fewer workers by increasing the rate of exploitation in increasing the length of the working day, increasing the intensity of work, or by decreasing the value of labour power; see Chapter 2.8. Notice that the assumption of a constant rate of surplus value has been relaxed. For a given rate of exploitation, total surplus values and total profits can increase only if more workers are employed.

> The number of labourers employed by capital, hence the absolute mass of the labour set in motion by it, and therefore the absolute mass of surplus labour absorbed by it, the mass of the surplus-value produced by it, and therefore the absolute mass of the profit produced by it, *can*, consequently, increase, and increase progressively, in spite of the progressive drop in the rate of profit. And this not only *can* be so. Aside from temporary fluctuations it *must* be so, on the basis of capitalist production.
>
> (*KIII*, Ch. XIII, p. 218)

The competitive nature of accumulation and its effect on the rate of profit, as argued by Marx, is illustrated by the following passages from *KIII*:

> A capitalist working with improved but not as yet generally adopted methods of production sells below the market-price, but above his individual price of production; his rate of profit rises until competition levels it out. During this equalisation period the second requisite, expansion of the invested capital, makes its appearance. According to the degree of this expansion the capitalist will be able to employ a part of his former labourers, actually perhaps all of them, or even more, under the new conditions, hence to produce the same, or a greater, mass of profit.
> (*KIII*, Ch. XIII, p. 231)

> No capitalist ever *voluntarily* introduces a new method of production, no matter how much more productive it may be, and how much it may increase the rate of surplus-value, so long as it reduces the rate of profit. Yet every such new method of production cheapens the commodities. Hence, the capitalist sells them originally above their prices of production or, perhaps, above their value. He pockets the difference between their costs of production and the market prices of the same commodities produced at higher costs of production. He can do this, because the average labour-time required socially for the production of these latter commodities is higher than the labour time required for the new methods of production. His method of production stands above the social average. But competition makes it general and subject to the general law. There follows a fall in the rate of profit — perhaps first in this sphere of production and eventually it achieves a balance with the rest — *which is, therefore, wholly independent of the will of the capitalist.*
> (*KIII*, Ch. XV, pp. 264–5, emphasis added)

It is clear from the above quotes that, for Marx, the falling rate of profit is due to the competitive nature of capitalism: each capitalist in attempting to maximise individual profits leads to a collective result which is unwanted! Let me now turn to the opposing forces of this Law.

6.4 Counteracting Influences

In the development of the Hegelian argument of the Law, Marx discusses various counteracting influences that convert the Law into a 'tendency'. The forces that lead to a falling rate of profit bring along concomitant counteracting forces. These counteracting influences are:

(i) *Increasing Intensity of Exploitation* The process of capital accumulation brings in machinery and division of labour. These factors increase the rate of surplus value by increasing the intensity of exploitation of labour power. Similarly, a lengthening of the working day increases the rate of exploitation.

(ii) *Depression of Wages below the Value of Labour Power* This is a cyclical factor that, say due to the IRA pushing wages below their value, increases the rate of exploitation. This is 'one of the most important factors checking the tendency of the rate of profit to fall' (*KIII*, Ch. XIV, p. 235). However, Marx argues that this does not belong in a 'general analysis of capital', but belongs to an 'analysis of competition' which is not dealt with in *Capital*.

(iii) *Cheapening of the Elements of Constant Capital* 'In short, the *same development* which increases the mass of the constant capital in relation to the variable reduces the *value* of its elements as a result of the increased productivity' (*KIII*, Ch. XIV, p. 236, emphasis added.).

(iv) *Relative Over-Population* Capital accumulation leads to redundancies in employment. This encourages new industries with relatively low organic compositions of capital and hence slows down the falling rate of profit.

(v) *Foreign Trade* This increases the rate of surplus value by lowering the value of labour power (because of cheaper food imports) and also lowers the value of constant capital. Together these forces tend to raise the rate of profit. Marx mentioned, but does not pursue, the idea that exports of capital to other countries may prevent the fall in the rate of profit.

To summarise, capital accumulation leads to a falling rate of profit. However, capital accumulation at the same time also leads to certain counteracting forces that convert the Law into a 'tendency'. Unlike the Classical School, the falling rate of profit is explained with *increasing* productivity and without resort to an increasing wage rate. Marx emphasises his results thus:

> We have thus seen in a general way that the same influences which produce a tendency in the general rate of profit to fall, also call forth counter-effects, which hamper, retard and partly paralyse this fall. The latter do not do away with the law, but impair its effect. Otherwise, it would not be the fall of the general rate of profit, but rather its relative slowness,

> that would be incomprehensible. Thus, the law acts only as a tendency. And it is only under certain circumstances and only after long periods that its effects become strikingly pronounced.
>
> (*KIII*, Ch. XIV, p. 239)

> The tendency of the rate of profit to fall is bound up with a tendency of the rate of surplus-value to rise, hence with a tendency for the rate of labour exploitation to rise. Nothing is more absurd, for this reason, than to explain the fall in the rate of profit by a rise in the rate of wages, although this may be the case by way of an exception . . . The rate of profit does not fall because labour becomes less productive, but because it becomes more productive. Both the rise in the rate of surplus-value and the fall in the rate of profit are but specific forms through which growing productivity of labour is expressed under capitalism.
>
> (*KIII*, Ch. XIV, p. 240)

6.5 Internal Contradictions of the Law

I shall deal with this only briefly in this chapter as I shall be discussing these issues more fully in Chapter 9 on Crises. The main internal contradiction of the Law is that accumulation leads to a falling rate of profit, and a falling rate of profit leads to accumulation, concentration and centralisation of capital. This leads to a contradiction between the production and realisation of surplus value. This in turn leads to crises.

Although Marx argues that capitalists are attempting to maximise profits (or surplus values), he says that the 'rate of profit is the goad of capitalist production' (*KIII*, Ch. XV, p. 241). The falling rate of profit thus presents capitalists with a frightening prospect. The falling rate of profit threatens the capitalist system itself.

6.6 Criticisms of the Law

Marx's Law of the tendency of the rate of profit to fall has been criticised on theoretical and empirical grounds. The theoretical criticisms are based on the following arguments: first, Marx's model does not logically imply a falling rate of profit; secondly, even if there were such an implication, it is inconsistent with other aspects of Marx's model; and thirdly, that Marx ignores realisation (effective demand) problems involved in the circulation process. The empirical evidence, it is argued, does not support Marx's contention of an increasing organic composition of capital and a falling rate of profit. These empirical criticisms will be dealt with in the next section. To appreciate some of the criticisms, the reader must keep in mind the three systems: commodity, value and price. In addition, the distinction between an individual capitalist and the capitalist class must also be kept in mind.

(i) *Marx's Model Does Not Imply a Falling Rate of Profit*

There are two strands to this argument: first, that there is no inevitable tendency for the organic composition of capital to rise and secondly, that technical change must lead to a *higher* rate of profit for a given real wage rate if capitalists are assumed to be rational in their behaviour.

(a) *Increasing Organic Composition of Capital*[3] Marx's argument is that during the process of capitalist development there would be increasing capital accumulation. He assumes that technological change, on balance, is labour saving. There are, of course, no theoretical reasons why this must be so. As far as capitalists are concerned they want to maximise profits; if a capital saving innovation decreases costs, then it would be employed. It is possible to argue that capitalists in order to increase their *social control* over workers would like to have a continual threat of redundancy hang over their heads. This, of course, would encourage labour saving technology.

Even assuming that technological change is labour saving, so that labour is replaced by machines (capital), it does not follow that the organic composition of capital in the *value system* will increase. In other words, the technical composition of capital (in the *commodity system*) may rise, but the organic composition of capital (in the *value system*) may not. This depends on technological change in the capital goods sector relative to the consumption (wage) goods sector. If there is technological change only in the capital goods sector, more machines may embody *less* labour and hence have a lower value. Marx argues that capitalists may attempt to reduce the value of labour power to increase the rate of exploitation by introducing technological change in the consumption (wage) sector. It is at this stage that Marx's distinctions between the various compositions of capital are relevant. As I mentioned in Chapter 2, Fine and Harris (1979) distinguish between the value composition of capital (VCC), the organic composition of capital (OCC) and the technical composition of capital (TCC). They argue that the VCC is at current values, while the OCC 'mirrors' the TCC. Hence when Marx argued that the OCC would rise, it was because the TCC was rising (at least in Marx's day).

The rate of profit, however, should really be defined in the price system. Thus we need to know what happens to the organic composition of capital in terms of prices of production. From our discussion of the transformation problem we know that prices are not proportional to values and hence, even if we know the trend of the TCC or OCC, we do not know how it varies in the price domain.

To summarise, there is no theoretical reason to expect an inevitable rise in the organic composition of capital.

(b) *Technical Change leads to a* Higher *Rate of Profit*[4] Neo-Ricardians argue that the effect of technological change is to *raise* the rate of profit in the price system, given a *constant real wage*. Okishio (1961) argues that, for a given real wage, if technical change lowers the unit cost of production (in the price system) then, at the new equilibrium set of prices, the rate of profit (in the price system) is either unchanged or it will *rise*. The rate of profit will remain unchanged if the technical change is in the luxury goods sector and it will *rise* if technical change is in the consumption (wage) goods sector or in the constant capital sector.[5] If the rate of profit falls, he argues, a profit seeking capitalist would not choose the new technique of production. Alternatively, if he found that the profit rate were lower he would return to the old technique, as long as the technical change was not irreversible. Schefold (1976) has shown that if technical change is of the type that *lowers* the labour coefficients but *raises* the coefficients of constant capital such that unit costs are lowered, then the *maximal* rate of profit must fall and the *maximal* real wage rate must rise. Let me illustrate the arguments by the use of a diagram called the factor-price frontier as shown in Diagram 6.1.

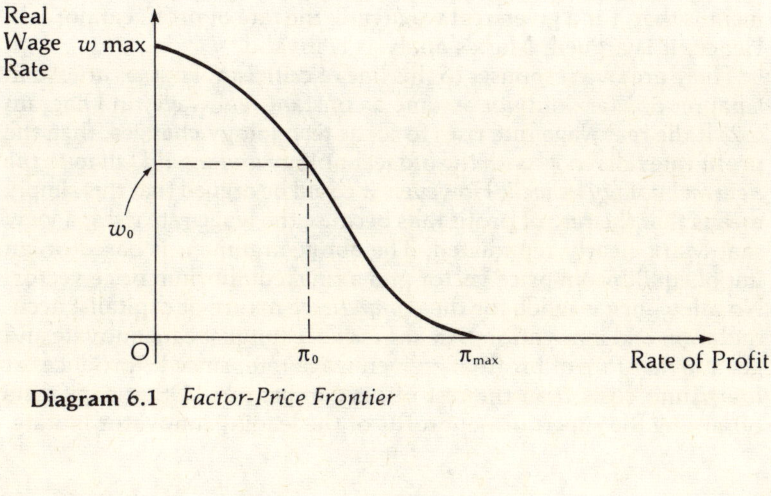

Diagram 6.1 *Factor-Price Frontier*

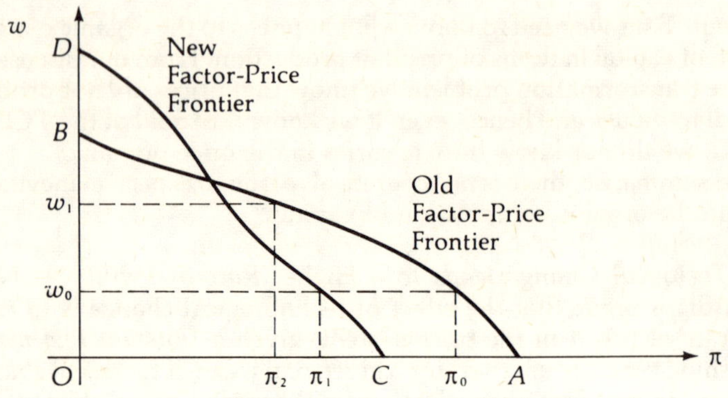

Diagram 6.2 *Technical Change and the Rate of Profit*

The factor-price frontier gives combinations of the real wage rate and the profit rate (in the price system) which are consistent with general equilibrium. For each real wage rate there is a maximum rate of profit which would be achieved in a competitive system. For example, in Diagram 6.1, for a real wage rate w_0, the competitive system would generate a profit rate of π_0. Now let a change in technology, of the type discussed above, occur. This is illustrated in Diagram 6.2.

In Diagram 6.2 *AB* is the old factor price frontier and *CD* the new one. Assume the real wage rate is w_0. Before the change in technology the rate of profit was π_0 and it has fallen to π_1. Clearly no capitalist would introduce the new technology if he foresaw the consequences of that change. If he did introduce the new technology, he would rapidly retreat (if possible) to the old technology *AB*. Thus the argument is that, for a given real wage rate, the rate of profit cannot fall. Hence, it is argued, Marx's analysis is invalid.

There are two responses to this line of criticism. First, as argued in Chapter 5, Marx did *not* assume a constant real wage. In Diagram 6.2, if the real wage rate rises to w_1 as technology changes, then the profit rate falls to π_2 with the old technology *and would fall with the new technology as well*. However, it could be argued that this simply means that the rate of profit falls because the wage rate rises, a view that Marx clearly repudiated. The above argument is based on an initial equilibrium price vector and a final equilibrium price vector. No allowance is made for the *competitive* nature of capitalist accumulation and innovation. An *individual* capitalist can innovate and get a *higher* rate of profit at a given wage rate, since he produces at *lower* unit costs than the rest of his competitors. Other capitalists observing the supernormal profits of the leading innovator imitate.

In the process they alter the price vector and collectively lead to the result of a *lower* profit rate which they did not foresee or desire! There is no social mechanism to lead to a cooperative result which may be in their collective interests. This is why Marx refers to the anarchic nature of capitalism.

(ii) *Constancy of the Rate of Exploitation*?[6]

In Chapter XIII of *KIII* Marx assumes a constant rate of exploitation, while in Chapter XIV he treats an increase in the rate of exploitation as a counteracting influence. However, technological change which necessarily accompanies capital accumulation leads to increasing productivity. If there is increasing productivity in the consumption goods sector (specifically in the basket of goods consumed by workers), it implies a fall in the value of labour power (in the value system) and hence an increase in the rate of exploitation. Thus an increase in the rate of exploitation is not merely a counteracting influence, but an integral part of the accumulation process. (Marx, of course, would not deny this accusation.) However, as he assumes constancy of the rate of exploitation in Chapter XIII, it implies that the real wage rate (in the commodity system) must increase so that the *value* of labour power is unchanged. But, it is argued, this is inconsistent with another part of Marx's model where a constant subsistence wage is the resultant of the IRA. As I argued in the last chapter, Marx assumes that the real wage rate is given at any point in time, but increases over time due to increasing productivity. Hence there is no contradiction.

Once we allow the rate of exploitation to vary, then what happens to the value rate of profit depends on the relative rates of increase of the organic composition of capital and the rate of exploitation. Marx, however, argues that the rate of exploitation cannot increase indefinitely because there is an insurmountable limit set by the 24 hour day. The maximum surplus value per worker is 24 hours if the value of labour power is zero. Of course, the rate of exploitation tends towards infinity as the value of labour power tends towards zero.

(iii) *Ignores Demand Factors*

Marx defines the rate of profit in the value system even though it is after he has discussed circulation in *KII* and the transformation problem in an earlier part of *KIII*. Marx attempts to demonstrate his

Law purely by looking at the system of production: it is independent of the process of circulation or distribution. Thus he ignores any Keynesian effective demand problems (which are *short-run* problems), as well as any distributional conflicts over wages and profits. Just as he would like to demonstrate the nature and existence of exploitation in 'pure' form at a high level of abstraction, he does the same with this Law. It is only when he discusses the internal contradictions that he combines production, circulation and distribution. I shall return to a discussion of this in Chapter 9 on Crises.

6.7 Evidence

Empirical tests of the Law are hampered by the unavailability of statistics on variables defined in a Marxian way. No data exist for the organic composition of capital, rate of surplus value, or for variables defined in terms of prices of production. The data are collected in terms of *market* prices. If we assume, as Marx does, that market prices fluctuate around prices of production, we can use the *trend* values of variables in the price system as an approximation to their prices of production.

There are certain conceptual and accounting problems involved in looking at the evidence. Let me take the conceptual problems first. In Section 6.2 I discussed some of the problems involved: are rents and interest included in total profits? Does the denominator include circulating capital? A more important difficulty is how we add together different kinds of capital (the aggregation problem): the normal procedure is simply to use a set of prices to obtain capital in the price system. However, as the reswitching debate emphasised, these prices are not independent of the distribution of income. Another difficulty is, how do we distinguish a cycle from a trend? What we may call a trend may be part of a longer cycle. Clearly, Marx's analysis refers to the long run: but how long is the long run? The answers to these problems are not easy and the empirical work tends to be pragmatic. Finally, what is the relation of the rate of profit in the price system to the internal rate of return? Feldstein and Summers (1977) show that under the assumption of a constant geometric rate of depreciation, the rate of return:

$$r = \frac{\text{Profits} - \text{Depreciation}}{\text{Net Capital Stock}}$$

which is similar to Marx's definition, except that circulating capital (Marx's variable capital plus expenditure on raw materials etc.) is excluded from the denominator. If depreciation is assumed to be of the 'one-hoss-shay' variety (capital goods have a constant efficiency for T periods and then suddenly collapse), then the rate of return is:

$$r = \frac{\text{Profits}}{\text{Gross Capital Stock}}$$

In both cases Profits include rents and interest.

The accounting problems involve the valuation of capital stock, the measurement of depreciation and the inclusion or exclusion of stock appreciation. There are problems of measuring capital stock: is it to be valued at historic costs or replacement costs? There are differences between different methods of measuring depreciation, such as constant geometric rates, straight-line depreciation, etc. Again, in inflationary periods stocks appreciate in nominal terms, so proper allowance has to be made for it.

The most quoted work in this field is Gillman's (1957) study on the rate of profit in the USA for the period 1849–1952. The results of the study did not show any long-term decline in the rate of profit. The study could not find any long-term increasing trend in the organic composition of capital. There are several problems with this study which are discussed in Desai (1979). I shall turn to looking briefly at a few British studies.

A controversial study by Glyn and Sutcliffe (1972) showed that the rate of profit in the UK for quoted companies in the industrial and commercial sector declined rapidly from 1967 to 1970, which is hardly a trend movement. However, they conclude that this fall in the rate of profits was not due to an increase in the organic composition of capital, but rather to increases in wages squeezing profits — a very un-Marxian result.[7] In a series of papers in the Bank of England Quarterly, Flemming *et al.* (1976 a & b), Clark and Williams (1978) have calculated the rate of profit for the post-war period in the UK. They find that there has been a significant decline in the rate of profit of Industrial and Commercial Companies (excluding North Sea Oil and Gas) from the mid-sixties until 1977. They are concerned about the implications for long-term investment of the dramatic fall in the rate of profit. They make no attempt to see to what extent this fall in the rate of profit is due to cyclical and trend factors.

To summarise, the rates of profit as measured by traditional economists differ from Marx's rate of profit. The evidence for the UK suggests that there has been a significant decline in the rate of profit since the mid-sixties. It is difficult to assess what role the organic composition of capital plays in this decline. It is also difficult to assess, without further work, to what extent cyclical factors explain this decline.

6.8 Assessment

Let me begin by summarising the discussion of this chapter. Marx argues that the value rate of profit *tends* to fall due to a rising organic composition of capital. There are counteracting influences which may 'hamper, retard and partly paralyse' this long-term trend. In reviewing the criticisms I touched upon the theoretical difficulty involved in predicting an increasing trend in the organic composition of capital. I also discussed the argument that no rational capitalist would introduce a new technique if it lowered the rate of profit. I argued that it was perfectly rational for an *individual* capitalist to introduce a new technique that gave him *temporarily* higher profits. As long as he is one step ahead it does not concern him that if everyone imitates him the rate of profit will fall. It simply reinforces Marx's arguments about the anarchic nature of capitalism. In discussing the assumption of the constancy of the rate of exploitation, I argued that Marx simply uses that assumption at a higher level of abstraction in his analysis. When he discusses counteracting influences the rate of exploitation is allowed to increase. These counteracting influences are part of the dialectical process. Finally, I reviewed some of the problems involved in looking at the evidence and commented on the inconclusive nature of the evidence available to date.

It is clear Marx considered this Law as a very important element in analysing capitalist economics. A falling rate of profit does have deleterious effects on accumulation and hence the development of capitalism. If accumulation slackens, we have a crisis. Let me end by quoting Marx:

> The progressive tendency of the general rate of profit to fall is, therefore, just *an expression peculiar to the capitalist mode of production* of the progressive development of the social productivity of labour.
>
> (*KIII*, Ch. XIII, p. 213)

Notes to Chapter 6

1. I am ignoring aggregation problems and the associated 're-switching' controversy. See Harcourt and Laing (1971) or Burmeister (1980).
2. Assuming that there is a unique internal rate of return. See Junankar (1972) for further details.

3. See Sweezy (1942), Meek (1967) and Fine and Harris (1979) Ch. 4 and the references cited therein.
4. See Okishio (1961), Steedman (1977), Roemer (1978), Schefold (1976), Shaikh (1978), (1980).
5. See Chapter 3.6.
6. See Robinson (1966), Sweezy (1942).
7. See Glyn and Harrison (1980).

Further Reading for Chapter 6

1. *KIII*, Chs II–V, XIII–XV
2. *Grundrisse* (1973) pp. 376–98 and 745–72.
3. *TSVII* Ch. XVI
4. Sweezy (1942)
5. Meek (1967)
6. Hodgson (1974)
7. Fine and Harris (1979) Ch. 4
8. Steedman (1977) Ch. 9

Money is therefore the god among commodities
(Grundrisse, p. 221)

7 Money and Circulation*

7.1 Introduction

In this chapter I shall review Marx's analysis of the role of money in the process of circulation (exchange) in a capitalist economy. After a long period of neglect, there has been a recent upsurge of interest in Marx's monetary theory. Superficially, Marx's theory is similar to the Classical Quantity Theory, as well as to Keynes' analysis in the *General Theory*. However, this superficial resemblance is wrong. Marx's monetary theory is set firmly in the context of *Capital* where the role of historical, social and political relations differentiates his work from Fisher and Friedman, Keynes and Clower. Marx's analysis of the role of money is, however, limited to the role of commodity money, with only minor digressions into paper or fiat money. In most of the discussion he assumes prices are equal to values and the reader is reminded that I shall retain this assumption throughout this chapter. For the purposes of exposition I shall follow the traditional order for discussing money: in Section 2 I discuss the Role of Money; in Section 3 the Demand for Money; in Section 4 the Supply of Money; in Section 5 Money and the Rate of Interest; in Section 6 Money, Circulation and Prices; and conclude briefly in Section 7.

---

*I am grateful to my colleagues Roy Bailey and Jeff Sheen for perceptive comments on this chapter. They are not responsible for remaining errors or prejudices.

7.2 Role of Money

As mentioned above, Marx usually identifies money with gold. Gold has several useful properties: it is homogeneous, divisible, easy to carry, has a high ratio of value to weight, and durability. By assumption, gold is produced at constant costs. For Marx, money (gold) is a unit of account, a medium of exchange, and a store of value. Unlike the Walrasian model, money plays an integral role in Marx's model. To understand the role of money, let me remind the reader about simple commodity production. (See Chapter 2.4.)

$$\hat{C}_1 \rightarrow M \rightarrow \hat{C}_2$$

where $\hat{C}_1$ are (a set of) commodities of type 1 which are sold for money, M, and *then* used to purchase (a set of) commodities $\hat{C}_2$. (Since I am assuming values = prices, I am ignoring the parentheses after the $\hat{C}$s.) Note that this is a *temporal* sequence, so that time enters the analysis in a significant way. Again, there may be a *spatial* difference between $\hat{C}_1$ and $\hat{C}_2$: $\hat{C}_1$ may be sold in London and $\hat{C}_2$ purchased in Colchester.

> But no one is forthwith bound to purchase, because he has just sold. Circulation bursts through all restrictions as to time, place and individuals imposed by direct barter, and this it effects by splitting up, into the antithesis of a sale and a purchase . . .
>
> (*KI*, Ch. III, p. 113)[1]

Let me emphasise certain important aspects of money as a medium of circulation. First, seen as a process of circulation we have two antithetical movements: the movement of commodities and the movement of money. Secondly, for money to circulate as a medium of exchange, it *must* have already performed its role as a unit of account. Compared to a barter economy where we would need to know thousands of relative prices, in a monetary economy we need to know the prices only in terms of money. An illustration may help.

Money is a unique commodity that exchanges with *all* commodities. In Table 7.1, the Xs refer to the possibilities of exchange and the Os refer to the impossibility of exchange. Thus money exchanges for *all* the commodities, while the commodities all exchange with money and only with themselves: $\hat{C}_1$ does not exchange for $\hat{C}_2$. In Clower's (1969) words, 'money buys goods, goods buy money, but goods do not buy goods.' In a barter economy there would be fewer zeros and hence we would need to know many more relative prices. In addition, we may have to go through a sequence of transactions to obtain the desired commodities. Thirdly, since the circulation of commodities

Table 7.1 Money and Circulation

	M	C_1	C_2	....	C_n
M	X	X	X		X
C_1	X	X	O		O
C_2	X	O	X		O
.	.				
.	.				
.	.				
.	.				
.	.				
C_n	X	O	O	....	X

involves time, money must be a store of value *at least* for a short period. If I sell some commodities in exchange for money, then until I buy some other commodities, I am holding on to it in the expectation that someone else will accept the money subsequently. Hence money uniquely combines the three functions of unit of account, medium of exchange and store of value.

Because of its primacy, money (gold) also acts as a commodity which is accumulated. On selling my commodities, I may hoard the money acquired. Under certain historical circumstances, the possibility of hoarding gold leads to a greed for its acquisition. Gold becomes a symbol of social and economic power. Under capitalist production, the process of circulation begins with money and ends with money; see Chapter 2.4. The capitalist begins with M and ends up with M'.

$$M \rightarrow \hat{C} \rightarrow M'$$

where M' is greater than M i.e. the surplus value created in the production process. Money, here, is money capital, i.e. money advanced by the capitalist to pay for constant and variable capital.

As discussed earlier, gold has become the universal equivalent as the result of a historical process. Marx tends to treat paper money as a 'symbol' for gold. However, there is a prescient remark:

> Gold circulates because it has value, whereas paper has value because it circulates.
>
> (*Critique*, p. 121)

The modern monetary system is based on the fundamental premise that money is acceptable because it circulates, or it circulates because it is acceptable. Or briefly, money is acceptable because it is acceptable! More accurately, money is acceptable because it is expected to be acceptable.

7.3 The Demand for Money

It is possible to discern a transactions demand and asset demand for money in Marx's writings. The transactions demand for money is due to the non-coincidence of receipts and payments.[2] Unlike traditional approaches to the transaction demand for money, Marx conceives of the demand for money as a medium of circulation as an 'involuntary' demand. During the process of circulation individuals sell commodities and, until they get around to buying other commodities, they hold money. The quantity of money held is dependent on various social and institutional features of trade.[3] There is a certain amount of money which is necessary for the circulation process, given the level of production of commodities. Production takes place, and commodities exchange according to their values. Money (gold) intermediates all transactions according to the value of gold: money acts both as a unit of account (measure of value) and as a medium of circulation. This view of the transactions demand for money contrasts with (say) the Cambridge equation ($M = kPY$, where k is determined by *individual* choice, P is the price level and Y is real national income). In his *Critical Essays*, Hicks (1967, p. 16) argues against the idea that the transactions demand for money is a voluntary choice variable:

> There is no 'Transactions Motive' behind it. It is the money that is needed to *circulate* a certain volume of goods, at a particular level of prices.

Although Hicks does not refer to him, Marx's argument is precisely the same. Clearly, the amount of money required to circulate a given quantity of commodities would depend on the velocity of circulation. To quote Marx:

> . . . the quantity of gold required for circulation is in the first place determined therefore by the sum of the commodity-prices to be realised. This sum, however, is in its turn determined by the following factors: 1. the price level . . . , and 2. the quantity of commodities circulating at definite prices . . .
>
> (*Critique*, p. 103)

> The velocity of circulation of gold can thus make up for its quantity . . .
> (*Critique*, p. 104)

As I shall return to this later, let me now turn to the asset demand for money. Since money is a store of value, people hoard it. In simple commodity production, if the sale of a commodity is not followed by a purchase, then the seller has sold a use value and obtained universal exchange value. He is able to purchase commodities in the future; its circuit of circulation is interrupted to provide this hoard. The possibility of hoarding money which provides exchange value for the future leads to 'greed' and 'avarice'. 'Thus social power becomes the private power of private persons' (*KI*, Ch. III, p. 132). These hoards provide a latent source of money for the ebbs and flows of trade. Since these hoards are for future purchases, their value rises or falls with changes in the value of gold. Implicitly, Marx assumes that gold is produced under constant costs. Change in technology may lead to a fall in its value. Money is hoarded because it is a medium of circulation for the future but, because it is hoarded, it is not in circulation. What determines the amounts of money hoarded? Marx's discussion of hoards, in simple commodity production, is in terms of greed, with little sophisticated analysis. However, it is clear that since these hoards are for *future* purchases, they must depend on *expectations* about the movements of values (prices) in the future.[4] The process of acquisition of hoards leads to changes in social relations, since some commodity producers become rich and acquire social power.

When we turn from simple commodity production to capitalist production ($M \rightarrow \hat{C} \rightarrow M'$), money is money capital. A capitalist continually strives to increase his profits and to add to his money capital stock. The capitalist purchases commodities with M, but in fact simply *advances* the money, since after production he sells the commodities and replaces the money advanced as well as making a profit. The amount of money demanded here depends on the level of capitalist development. In *KIII* there is a discussion of the relationship between money and the interest rate, some of which is (superficially) very Keynesian.

> Since a rise in interest implies a fall in the price of securities, this simultaneously offers a fine opportunity to people with available money-capital, to acquire at ridiculously low prices such interest-bearing securities as must, in the course of things, at least regain their average price as soon as the rate of interest falls again.
> (*KIII*, Ch. XXII, p. 361)

This sounds exactly like Keynes' speculative demand for money. (I shall return to money and the interest rate in Section 7.5.)

To summarise this section, money demand may be conceived of as an asset demand and an involuntary demand as a medium of circulation. The transactions demand appears to be like the Quantity equation and the asset demand has some Keynesian features.

7.4 The Supply of Money

The supply of money consists of gold, paper money and credit. The value of gold, like any other commodity, is determined by the socially necessary labour embodied in it. The production of gold is determined by profit maximising capitalists. (Remember that gold is produced under constant costs.) Gold, however, is a unique commodity in that it has (virtually) no use value, but has exchange value. The amount of gold produced is then determined by the circumstances of the circulation process. Since all commodities in a monetary economy are traded for money, there has to be a sufficient quantity available for these trades to be effected. Given the velocity of circulation, the quantity of gold is determined by the price level and the production of commodities. To quote Marx:

> . . . the quantity of the circulating medium is determined by the sum of the prices of the commodities, and the average velocity of currency . . .
> (*KI*, Ch. III, p. 123)

Note that this is in direct contrast to the Quantity theorists, about which more later. Paper money is simply used to replace gold in circulation. Paper money is simply a 'symbol' representing gold. To quote Marx:

> The issue of paper money must not exceed in amount the gold (or silver as the case may be) which would actually circulate if not replaced by symbols.
> (*KI*, Ch. III, pp. 127–8)

If there is too much paper money then it might 'fall into general disrepute' and represent only that quantity of gold that is required, i.e. paper money depreciates.

Marx has only a brief analysis of credit. The amount of credit is determined by the development of the banking system and the level of development of capitalist production. Credit simply increases the velocity of circulation. (See *KIII*, Ch. XXVII.)

7.5 Money and Interest

Marx's analysis of money and the interest rate is incomplete, but a brief review would be helpful. Interest payments to money capitalists are subtractions from surplus value that is created in the production process. Thus interest income is determined by a conflict between industrial capitalists and money capitalists: between different 'fractions' of capital in the circulation process. The maximum amount of total interest payments are obtained when they equal surplus value. The minimum is zero (assuming no inflation). Marx seems to imply that there is an indeterminacy in total interest payments. As regards the interest *rate*, Marx argues that there is no 'natural rate of interest' (analogous say to equilibrium prices of commodities). There is no natural rate of interest, because interest is a phenomenon which occurs in the sphere of *circulation*; money capital has use value to the borrower but has no *value* and hence no 'price of production'. (Note here we are referring to money capital and not money.) Long-run equilibrium prices are determined by the amount of socially necessary labour; money capital is not produced, hence it has no equilibrium price.

It is interesting to note that the discussion of the interest rate is mainly in terms of borrowing by industrial capitalists from money capitalists. The borrowing and lending by the working class is ignored, except in references to workers borrowing from pawnshops. If workers are paid their value of labour power, can they save? Harris (1976) argues that since workers have to reproduce themselves, the value of labour power must allow an element for providing for dependent members in the family, the young, the old and those who are in the IRA. Hence, savings are *necessary* for the working class. (Since Marx is considering a growing economy with technological change there are positive savings for the working class.) These savings are mobilised by the banking system for the capitalist class.

To return to the interest rate, as there is no natural rate, what determines the market rate of interest? For Marx the market rate of interest is determined by the demand and supply for money capital. It is important to note that the rate of interest is determined not by the demand and supply of money, but by the demand and supply of money *capital*. It is only the amounts of money capital that are demanded by industrial capitalists and amounts supplied by money capitalists that determine the rate of interest. To quote Marx:

> . . . the relation between the supply of loanable capital on one side and the demand for it on the other, decides the market level of interest at any given time.
>
> (*KIII*, Ch. XXII, p. 366)

> Interest is a relationship between two capitalists, not between capitalist and labourer.
>
> (*KIII*, Ch. XXIII, p. 382)

As argued in Chapter 6, Marx postulated a falling rate of profit. As interest payments come out of profits which are created in the production process, Marx argued that the rate of interest would be 'regulated' by the rate of profit. Since there is a tendency for the rate of profit to fall, so there is a tendency for the rate of interest to fall.

> In any event the average rate of profit is to be regarded as the ultimate determinant of the maximum limit of interest.
>
> (*KIII*, Ch. XXII, p. 360)

> Since we have seen that the rate of profit is inversely proportional to the development of capitalist production, it follows that the higher or lower rate of interest in a country is in the same inverse proportion to the degree of industrial development . . .
>
> (*KIII*, Ch. XXII, p. 359)

Besides the explanation of the long-term falling rate of interest in terms of the rate of profit, two other reasons are brought forward. First, as capitalism develops, the *rentier* class grows and the supply of loanable funds increases relative to demand. Secondly, the development of the credit and banking system extends the access to money capital.

Besides the trend movements in the interest rate, Marx commented on its cyclical nature:

> . . . a low rate of interest generally corresponds to periods of prosperity or extra profit, a rise in interest separates prosperity and its reverse, and a maximum of interest up to a point of extreme usury corresponds to the period of crisis.
>
> (*KIII*, Ch. XXII, p. 361)

> The rate of interest reaches its peak during crises, when money is borrowed at any cost to meet payments.
>
> (*KIII*, Ch. XXII, p. 362)

The cyclical nature of the interest rate is due to contradictory aspects of the demand for money capital: the demand for money capital for expansion and the demand for money capital for liquidity. He postulated that this demand for liquidity (to be able to meet commitments) would be the major influence and hence explain the cyclical changes in interest rate. However, given these contradictory forces, it would be possible to observe 'low interest to go along with stagnation and for moderately rising interest to go along with revived activity' (*KIII*, Ch. XXII, p. 361).

7.6 Money, Circulation and Prices

Marx's analysis of the role of money in circulation and its relation to the price level in some ways ante-dates Keynes, Clower and Leijonhufvud. His criticism of (what is now called) Say's Law and Walras' Law, and the Quantity Theory has many important analytical features.

As mentioned earlier, there is an important difference between a barter economy and a monetary economy. In a monetary economy, money intermediates between all transactions. Since money is a medium of circulation and a store of value, it is possible to separate (over time and space) the act of selling from the act of buying. Thus in a barter economy an act of selling also represents a demand for commodities and there can be no overall excess demand in the system: Say's Law holds. However, in a monetary economy there is the possibility of an excess demand (or supply) of *commodities* appearing. The *ex post* identity that total sales equal total purchases holds when we include money as one of the commodities. Marx (very correctly) criticises Say's Law on this basis. Because money is a store of value there can be an accumulation of hoards, so that although people sell, they do not buy immediately: they hold money which can be used to purchase commodities at some indeterminate time in the future.[5] However, the act of saving does not provide the producers with any correct 'signals' about how they should plan production.

Let me turn to the relation between money and prices: a relation that *appears* to be identical to the Quantity Theory. However, there are several differences between Marx's theory and the Quantity Theory. Let me begin by outlining Marx's theory before making a comparison.

First let me assume that gold has developed into money and that no paper money exists. Gold has a value determined like all commodities. Commodities that are produced are brought into circulation with a known value which is then 'measured' by gold and then as a medium of circulation, it is exchanged for it. Hence commodities enter the circulation process with a *pre-determined* price. As discussed earlier, given prices and a level of production a certain quantity of gold (money) is required to circulate the commodities, given a velocity of circulation. (The velocity of circulation is determined by socio-historical circumstances.) Here prices are *not* determined by the quantity of money (gold). Now assume that due to technological change in gold production, more gold is produced and its value (in the Marxian sense, of course) falls. If nothing else has changed (i.e. the level of production, values of commodities and velocity are constant), then the prices of commodities rise and more gold is needed to circulate them. But prices rise because the measure of value function (unit of account) of gold has changed, not because the medium of circulation has increased. If instead the value of gold is assumed constant and there is an increase in its supply (say, due to an exogenous increase in gold from abroad), other things remaining equal, then all that happens is that the 'excess supply' of gold does not circulate: it is hoarded. An increase in money supply does not have to increase prices, if money is a store of value. There are several passages in *KI*, Ch. III and the *Critique* to justify this interpretation. For example:

> Prices are thus high or low not because more or less money is in circulation, but there is more or less money in circulation because prices are high or low.
>
> (*Critique*, p. 105)

Now assume that the State issues inconvertible paper money. Further assume (as Marx appears to) that this paper money is a partial money: it is a medium of circulation, but not a store of value. (At any moment someone must be holding paper money, or it must be a temporary store of value.) Clearly, in this case an increase in paper money supply forces up the price level, as paper money depreciates due to increased supply.

> The rise or fall of commodity-prices corresponding to an increase or decrease in the volume of paper notes — the latter where paper notes are the sole medium of circulation — is accordingly merely a forcible assertion by the process of circulation of a law which was mechanically infringed by extraneous action; i.e. the law that the quantity of gold in circulation is determined by the prices of commodities and the volume of tokens of value in circulation is determined by the amount of gold currency which they replace in circulation.
>
> (*Critique*, p. 121)

In modern times, gold is no longer a medium of circulation and paper money is a store of value. Under these circumstances, an increase in paper money may simply add to a hoard and not influence prices. Marx criticises Hume's Quantity Theory both on theoretical and empirical grounds. He chides Hume for implying that all increases in money would necessarily circulate.

However, once we are in a State inconvertible paper money system, where paper is a medium of circulation and a store of value, commodities that enter the circulation process have a determinate value, but cannot be compared with a money commodity with a value. (Paper money is assumed to have negligible value.) The price level is not determinate in the sense that any level of paper money would give a different price level.

Let me now turn to a brief comparison of the Quantity Theory and Marx's theory of money. Superficially they are very similar. They both assume that velocity is determined by institutional constraints. They both argue that increases (decreases) in money supply do not have any 'real' effects on output and employment. However, the Quantity theorist has a full employment model; Marx has a model with unemployment which fluctuates with changes in aggregate demand. For the Quantity theorist, the quantity of money determines prices; for Marx the level of prices determines the quantity of money necessary for circulation. For the Quantity theorist all money circulates; for Marx hoarding may interrupt the circulation process.

7.7 Summary and Conclusions

Marx's analysis of the role of money is incomplete and at times inconsistent. However, he makes several important contributions to the analysis of a monetary economy. By introducing the store of value function of money, he differentiates between a barter economy and a monetary economy. The possibility of hoarding also brings in the possibility of crises; see Chapter 9. Marx anticipates Clower's 'dual decision hypothesis' in arguing that unless we sell commodities first, we cannot demand commodities.[6] Marx's analysis of the transactions demand for money forms an interesting contrast with traditional (bourgeois) analyses. Surprisingly, Hicks supports (without knowing it?) Marx's analysis. Marx's analysis of an asset demand for money has some similarities with Keynesian analysis. However, he does not pursue his comment on liquidity preference. His analysis of the determination of interest rates is clearly incomplete and requires further development. Marx's analysis of the relation between money and prices is very clearly an anti-Quantity Theory. However, with paper money his analysis is again incomplete.

It is worth reminding the reader that Marx's analysis of money has to be read in the context of the labour theory of value and the general materialistic account of society. The demands for money are not individual demands determined by utility maximising. They are determined by social and historical factors. To conclude, although there are some similarities with (especially) Keynesian analysis, Marx's monetary theory is significantly different.

Notes to Chapter 7

1. Also see *Critique*, p. 93.
2. See *KI*, Ch. III, p. 142.
3. Also see *Critique*, p. 147.
4. See *Critique*, p. 148
5. See *Critique*, p. 97
6. '. . . during certain stages of the commercial crisis of 1857/58 there were indeed more buyers than sellers of *one* commodity, i.e. *money*, and more sellers than buyers as regards *all other forms of money*, i.e. commodities. The metaphysical equilibrium of purchases and sales is confined to the fact that every purchase is a sale and every sale is a purchase, but this gives poor comfort to the possessors of commodities who, unable to make a sale, cannot accordingly make a purchase either.'
   (*Critique*, p. 97)

Further Reading for Chapter 7

1. *KI* Ch. III
2. *KIII* Parts IV and V
3. *Grundrisse*, Chapter on Money (especially pp. 146–151, 186–238)
4. *Critique* Ch. 2
5. Hicks (1967) Chs 1–3
6. Harris (1976)
7. Foley (1975)
8. de Brunhoff (1973)
9. Clower (1969)
10. Hussain (1975)

The question, then, is not where the surplus-value comes from but whence the money comes into which it is turned.
(*KII*, Ch. XVII, p. 330)

8 Money, Circulation and Models of Reproduction

8.1 Introduction

In Volume 2 of *Capital*, Marx discusses the 'Process of Circulation of Capital'. After examining the three circuits of capital (money capital, productive capital and commodity capital) he turns to analyse models of simple and extended reproduction. The importance of *KII* lies in the elaboration of a system of general equilibrium with money intermediating all transactions. Following in the footsteps of Quesnay's pathbreaking *Tableau Economique*, Marx analyses circular flow relationships of a stationary and growing economy. It is important to remember that Marx is analysing the process of *circulation*, not production. Given that he has already shown in *KI* that surplus value is created in the production process, he turns to analyse how in a money economy this surplus value is 'realised'. The main purpose of *KII* is to show the conditions of exchange (circulation) that are consistent with (or accommodate) a two sector stationary or expanding economy. His primary concern in his model of extended reproduction is *not* to analyse the conditions that lead to a steady state growth path, but to show that even in a growing economy money can (and does) intermediate all transactions. This interpretation of Marx's models of reproduction is at variance with the traditional interpretations which treat these models as steady state *growth* models. These interpretations pose a puzzle: why does Marx not discuss cyclical properties (crises) in *KII*. They also pose a puzzle over the peculiar behaviour assumed for capitalist accumulation. However, if my interpretation is accepted, then there is no puzzle: Marx is analysing conditions of *circulation* in a growth context, he is *not* analysing the process of growth.

It is worth stressing that Marx is *not* analysing an exchange economy (in the traditional economics sense) where no production is taking place: he is not analysing an abstract economy of individuals with given endowments of commodities. Marx is analysing a capitalist economy where production takes place by profit seeking (maximising) capitalists. He is analysing the conditions of circulation (exchange) that permit (or accommodate) capitalist production processes. He is analysing various inter-Departmental, inter-class, intra-Department and intra-*capitalist* class trades that take place in a capitalist economy.

Let me outline the remainder of this chapter. In Section 2, I shall explain Marx's circuits of capital: this is an analysis of the circuits of *individual* capitals (micro). In Section 3 I discuss Marx's model of simple reproduction: an analysis of circuits of social capital (macro) in a stationary economy. In Section 4 I outline the model of extended reproduction: a model of circulation in an economy growing at a steady state. Section 5 concludes with some general remarks. Throughout this chapter, following Marx, I shall assume that no technological change takes place and that commodities exchange at their values: in other words values equal prices.

8.2 Circuits of Capital

In Chapters 1 to 4 of *KII* Marx discusses the circuits of capital in a capitalist economy. He analyses the movement of individual capitals (micro) from exchange to production to exchange as a continuous process. The differentiating feature of a capitalist economy is that production is for exchange, not for use. In this process money plays a key role. Marx distinguishes three circuits of capital, the money capital circuit, the productive capital circuit and, finally, the commodity capital circuit.

(a) *The Money Capital Circuit*

This circuit begins with the capitalist advancing money capital to purchase labour power and material products (raw materials). Circulation is now interrupted and production takes place and new commodities that embody surplus value are produced. These commodities are then exchanged for a larger sum of money than before production took place: surplus value emerges as profit. Schematically:

$$M \rightarrow \hat{C} \begin{cases} L \\ MP \end{cases} \ldots \hat{P} \ldots \hat{C}' \rightarrow M'$$

where M denotes money capital, $\hat{C}$ commodities, L labour power, MP material products, $\hat{P}$ productive capital, $\hat{C}'$ new commodities produced and M' is the money received at the end of the process, including surplus value. Note that all variables are measured in values and hence I am ignoring the V in parentheses. The arrows indicate exchanges with money and the dots indicate that the circulation process is interrupted by production. Let me emphasise the following aspects of this circuit. First, the capitalist begins with money capital facing a propertyless proletariat. Labour power is a commodity. The capitalist uses his money capital to buy labour power (an inter-class transaction), as well as material products from other capitalists (an intra-class transaction). Money capital has been transformed into productive capital, $\hat{P}$, of the same value but of different form. Secondly, production now takes place interrupting the circuit: production takes place, surplus value is created and a certain length of time elapses before a set of commodities $\hat{C}'$ is produced. Surplus value is embodied in $\hat{C}'$: $\hat{C}'$ is greater in value (and different in form) from $\hat{C}$. These commodities are exchanged for a greater amount of money than was advanced by the capitalist. Thus this circuit emphasises that the aim of the capitalist is exchange value. The process of production appears as an 'unavoidable intermediate link' or a 'necessary evil' for the sake of making profits. This circuit of money capital continues with M' being the beginning of a new circuit.

In this circuit of money capital the capitalist makes only productive consumption: purchasing MP and L. The workers sell their labour power, obtain money and then purchase their subsistence basket of goods. This circulation of commodities, $L \rightarrow M \rightarrow \hat{C}$ is a premise of capitalist production: the worker has to reproduce his labour power. These transactions involving consumption by workers, as well as the consumption of commodities by capitalists *qua* consumption goods, is not included in the circuit of capitals.

(b) *The Productive Capital Circuit*

This circuit is described schematically as:

$\hat{P} \ldots \hat{C}' \rightarrow M' \rightarrow \hat{C} \ldots \hat{P}'$

Here the circuit of capital is viewed as beginning with productive capital $\hat{P}$ which then goes through a production process to produce commodities $\hat{C}'$ which embody surplus value. These commodities are exchanged for money; surplus value is realised as profits. The capitalist may now consume *all* of the surplus value, in which case production continues at the same level and $\hat{P} = \hat{P}'$. This is the case of simple reproduction. Alternatively, the capitalist may accumulate *all* of the surplus value in which case $\hat{P}' > \hat{P}$ and we have a case of expanded production. Normally we assume that the capitalist accumulates a certain proportion of surplus value. The circuit of productive capital, then, 'signifies the periodical renewal of the functioning of productive capital . . . aiming at the self expansion of value' (*KII*, Ch. II, p. 63).

For this circuit to continue smoothly and without interruption, $\hat{C}'$ must be sold at its value and M' must be exchanged for commodities. If there are any indivisibilities in buying new capital goods, the surplus value has to be hoarded and hence leads to a temporary break in the circuit.

Notice the following: first, circulation (or exchange) appears as a means of continuing the process of production and reproduction. Second, the *possibility* of a break in the circuit exists at different points.

(c) *The Commodity Capital Circuit*

This is represented schematically as:

$\hat{C} \rightarrow M' \rightarrow \hat{C} \ldots \hat{P} \ldots \hat{C}''$

where in simple reproduction (stationary state) $\hat{C}' = \hat{C}''$ and, in a growing economy, $\hat{C}'' > \hat{C}'$. The focus on commodities raises questions of how in aggregate these commodities are consumed by different social classes: by the workers for subsistence and by the capitalists for consumption and accumulation.

The three circuits of capital can be represented schematically as a continuous process:

Production Circulation (Exchange)

$$[M \rightarrow \hat{C} \ldots \vdots\, \hat{P} \ldots \{\hat{C}' \rightarrow M'] \rightarrow \hat{C} \ldots \hat{P}\,\vdots \ldots \hat{C}'\} \rightarrow$$

where [ ] contains the circuit of money capital, $\vdots\ \vdots$ contains the circuit of productive capital and { } contains the circuit of commodity capital. In this form it is easy to see that each circuit of capital is a 'unity of the processes of production and circulation' (*KII*, Ch. IV, p. 100).

Each circuit, in some sense, represents the same process. However, each has different emphases. The money circuit shows that capitalists aim to increase their money capital; M' is always greater than M. However, the surplus value is created in the production process and *appears* to result from the process of circulation (exchange). The productive capital circuit focuses on production and the expansion of production in an apparently objective fashion: the aim appears to be to increase production at minimum cost. However, it neglects the peculiar properties of money and money capital. Similarly, in the commodity circuit the role of profit is ignored.

In the productive capital and commodity capital circuits the process can continue at the same level with $\hat{P}' = \hat{P}$ and $\hat{C}' = \hat{C}$ (i.e. in a simple reproduction). However, in the money capital circuit the process *may* continue: the capitalist may withdraw from the process. The productive and commodity capital circuits are, in some sense, incomplete: they must continue to obtain money, since the aim of a capitalist is to maximise profits. The capitalist has to sell commodities to realise his profits.

8.3 Simple Reproduction

This is a general equilibrium model of an economy in a stationary state. Unlike the traditional general equilibrium model, money is not just a 'veil'. Money plays a crucial role in intermediating all transactions, and money capital plays an important role in the process of capitalist production. Again, in contrast to traditional general equilibrium theory, Marx analyses the domination of the capitalist class over the working class. The model is a two-sector, two-class model of a monetary economy. The question that Marx poses is, if an economy is to continue in a stationary state, what transactions must take place between and within sectors (departments) and between and within classes? What role does money play in this process? The model Marx analyses is of the circular flow of a macro economy: the movement of social capital.

The main question that Marx is attempting to answer, in the context of a stationary (or growing) economy, is:

> how is it possible that every capitalist draws a surplus-value in money out of the annual product, i.e., draws more money out of the circulation than he throws into it, since in the long run the capitalist class itself must be regarded as the source of all the money thrown into circulation?
>
> (*KII*, Ch. XX, p. 473)

Marx returns to this theme at several points in *KII*; in aggregate, *where* does the money come from to realise the surplus value? Perhaps we do not consider it an important question, but for Marx it is crucial to show that, since surplus value is created in production, the process of circulation is consistent with realising this surplus value. His answer is extremely simple: the circular flow of income and the velocity of circulation allow this realisation of surplus value.[1]

> The general reply has already been given: If a mass of commodities worth *x* times £1,000 has to circulate, it changes absolutely nothing in the quantity of the money required for this circulation whether the value of this mass of commodities contains any surplus-value or not, whether this mass of commodities has been produced capitalistically or not. *The problem itself therefore does not exist*. All other conditions being given, such as velocity of the currency of money, etc., a definite sum of money is required in order to circulate commodities worth *x* times £1,000 quite independently of how much or how little of this value falls to the share of the direct producers of these commodities. So far as any problem exists here, it coincides with the general problem: Where does the money required for the circulation of the commodities of a country come from?
>
> (*KII*, Ch. XVII, p. 333)

Let me now turn to a formal presentation of the model of simple reproduction:

Assumptions of Simple Reproduction Model[2]

These assumptions are as follows:

(i) There are only two classes: capitalists and workers;
(ii) The organic compositions of capital are constant over time, but may differ from each other;

$$q_1(V) \neq q_2(V)$$

(iii) Even though organic compositions of capital are different, goods exchange at their values. The transformation problem is ignored;

(iv) The production process is a point-input, point-output process. Each Department's technology is 'productive';

(v) There are constant returns to scale and no technical change;

(vi) There are two Departments: Department I Capital goods
Department II Consumption goods.

Department II consists of two sub-Departments: (a) necessities consumed by workers and capitalists; and (b) luxury goods consumed *only* by capitalists. These 'goods' are, of course, 'commodities' in Marx's sense. Intra-Departmental industries are aggregated, implicitly, by using values as weights;

(vii) There is a unit turnover period of capital;

(viii) Capitalists' net saving and investment are zero. Replacement investment is *within* the Department;

(ix) Wage rate is at subsistence level, so workers do not save;

(x) The rate of exploitation is constant and equal in the two Departments;

(xi) There is a closed economy.

Note: There would be different (value) profit rates if $q_1(V) \neq q_2(V)$.

Equilibrium in the Simple Reproduction Model

$$c_1(V) + v_1(V) + s_1(V) = w_1(V) \quad \text{Department I (Capital)}$$

$$c_2(V) + v_2(V) + s_2(V) = w_2(V) \quad \text{Department II (Consumption)}$$

The first equation states that constant capital of $c_1(V)$ plus variable capital of $v_1(V)$ produces an output of value $w_1(V)$, which exceeds the value of inputs by the amount of surplus value $s_1(V)$, in the Capital goods Department. Similarly, for Department II.

Capitalists of each Department have money capital with which they *advance* the wages payment for variable capital and constant capital. Thus money plays the role of store of value (as money capital) and medium of exchange in purchasing c and v. Since prices are assumed equal to values (or proportional to values), I shall omit the parentheses containing V in the remainder of this chapter.

For a stationary state economy there is no net increase in its capital stock and production continues at the same rate from year to year. In a two-Departmental economy we require that the production of each Department be unchanging. Capitalists of Department I produce capital goods, so that they and the workers must trade with Department II to provide them with the basic necessities and to provide the capitalists with luxury goods. In other words, Department I provides $v_1 + s_1$ of capital goods to Department II and purchases consumption goods of (equal) value c_2. Capitalists of Department I spend c_1 within their own Department on maintaining capital intact (replacement investment), in order to maintain a constant rate of production in the future. They spend their surplus value s_1 on purchasing consumer goods from Department II. The workers in Department I sell their labour power to the capitalists of that Department and then spend v_1 on buying consumer goods from Department II. Department II capitalists spend their surplus value s_2 within the Department. The workers in Department II sell their labour power to 'their' capitalists and then purchase from them consumer goods of value v_2. To maintain their capital intact, capitalists of Department II have to buy capital goods worth c_2 in value from Department I capitalists. Thus assuming a stationary state and voluntary and fair exchange, equilibrium requires that $v_1 + s_1$ of Department I's capital goods are exchanged for c_2 of Department II's consumption goods.

Formally, given

$$c_1 + \boxed{v_1 + s_1} = w_1$$

$$\boxed{c_2} + v_2 + s_2 = w_2$$

equilibrium requires

$$c_1 + c_2 = w_1 = c_1 + v_1 + s_1$$

(Demand for Capital goods = Supply of Capital goods) or, by elimination,

$$c_2 = v_1 + s_1$$

Similarly,

$$v_1 + s_1 + v_2 + s_2 = w_2\, c_2 + v_2 + s_2$$

(Demand for Consumption goods = Supply of Consumption goods) or, by elimination,

$$v_1 + s_1 = c_2$$

that is, both conditions reduce to the same equilibrium condition. (This is due to Walras' law: if $n - 1$ markets are in equilibrium, the nth market also clears.)

The equilibrium condition simply states that the value of capital goods sold by Department I must equal the value of consumption goods sold by Department II. Thus these intra- and inter-Departmental trades (as well as the intra- and inter-class trades) permit the realisation of surplus values created in the two Departments via the use of money as the medium of circulation.

> ... *thus the money thrown into circulation by this very department turns its own surplus value into money.*
>
> (*KII*, Ch. XX, p. 149, emphasis in original)

Thus in an economy with free and fair exchange, capitalists create surplus value in the production process and then realise it in the process of circulation through the means of money acting as a medium of exchange. The creation and realisation of surplus value has been masked by the process of circulation.

8.4 Extended Reproduction

As mentioned in the Introduction to this chapter, Marx analyses the role of money in a growing economy. He is interested in showing how surplus value created in an economy is realised and then provides for capital accumulation and hence growth. Again the focus is *not* on growth, but on how money accommodates the growth process via its role in capital accumulation. A growing economy requires additional money for circulation and this additional money comes via two sources (a) increased gold production and (b) increased velocity of circulation. The increases in velocity come about as a result of greater economy in the use of money and the running down of hoards.[3]

As in the case of simple reproduction, surplus value created in production is realised in the process of circulation via the inter- and intra-departmental trade flows. Capitalists advance money capital, buy labour power and constant capital. The surplus value created is partly consumed and partly saved. The savings are initially accumulated as latent (or virtual) money capital: a temporary hoard for accumulation. Due to indivisibilities in capital goods, capitalists have to accumulate a certain amount of money before being able to purchase a capital good. Any sudden changes in hoarding disrupt the circular flow and lead to under-/over-production.

Let me now turn to a formal presentation of Marx's model of extended reproduction, followed by a numerical illustration. This is a model of balanced growth equilibrium. We retain all the assumptions of Simple Reproduction *except* assumption (viii) which is replaced by

(viii)(a) Department I capitalists consume half of their surplus value and *invest the remainder in Department I.*

(b) Department II capitalists invest in Department II *as much as is required to remain in equilibrium.* They are passive adjusters.

(c) The investment in each Department is such as to leave the organic compositions of capital unchanged.

Assumption (ix) is extended to assume explicitly an infinitely elastic supply of labour at the subsistence wage rate.[4]

The capitalists of Department I use their surplus value (s_1) for consumption of 'wage and luxury goods' (s_{13}) for adding to constant capital in their Department (Δc_1 or s_{11}) and for adding to variable capital in their Department (Δv_1 or s_{12}) so as to keep q_1 constant, thus:

$$q_1 = \frac{c_1}{v_1} = \frac{c_1 + \Delta c_1}{v_1 + \Delta v_1} = \frac{\Delta c_1}{\Delta v_1} \qquad \text{(constant)}$$

$$s_1 \equiv s_{11} + s_{12} + s_{13} \equiv \Delta c_1 + \Delta v_1 + s_{13}$$

Similarly in Department II

$$q_2 = \frac{c_2}{v_2} = \frac{c_2 + \Delta c_2}{v_2 + \Delta v_2} = \frac{\Delta c_2}{\Delta v_2} \qquad \text{(constant)}$$

$$s_2 \equiv s_{21} + s_{22} + s_{23} \equiv \Delta c_2 + \Delta v_2 + s_{23}$$

Writing the model algebraically:

$$c_1 + v_1 + \Delta c_1 + \Delta v_1 + s_{13} = w_1$$

$$c_2 + v_2 + \Delta c_2 + \Delta v_2 + s_{23} = w_2$$

Equilibrium requires the output (supply) of capital goods to equal the demand i.e.:

$$\underbrace{c_1 + \Delta c_1 + c_2 + \Delta c_2}_{\text{(demand)}} = w_1 = \underbrace{c_1 + v_1 + \Delta c_1 + \Delta v_1 + s_{13}}_{\text{(supply)}}$$

or

$$c_2 + \Delta c_2 = v_1 + \Delta v_1 + s_{13}$$

Similarly, for the consumption goods Department:

$$\underbrace{v_1 + \Delta v_1 + s_{13} + v_2 + \Delta v_2 + s_{23}}_{\text{(demand)}} = w_2 = \underbrace{c_2 + v_2 + \Delta c_2 + \Delta v_2 + s_{23}}_{\text{(supply)}}$$

$$v_1 + \Delta v_1 + s_{13} = c_2 + \Delta c_2$$

This inter-Department trade can be shown:

$$c_1 + \Delta c_1 + \boxed{v_1 + \Delta v_1 + s_{13}}$$
$$\boxed{c_2 + \Delta c_2} + v_2 + \Delta v_2 + s_{23}$$

A numerical illustration may help to explain the conditions of equilibrium in a growing economy.

A Numerical Example of Extended Reproduction

Initial Period Year 'O'

	c	v	s	w	q
I	4000	1000	1000	6000	4
II	1500	750	750	3000	2
				9000	

Department I accumulates $\frac{1}{2}s_1 = 500$ of which

$\Delta c_1 = 4/5 \times 500 = 400$

$\Delta v_1 = 1/5 \times 500 = 100$

Department I capitalists consume $\frac{1}{2}s_1 = 500 = s_{13}$

Department II capitalists accumulate just enough constant capital so that demand and supply of capital goods are equal, which is $6000 - 4400 - 1500 = w_1 - (c_1 + \Delta c_1) - c_2 = 100 = \Delta c_2$. To keep q_2 constant, Department II must have $\Delta v_2 = 50$. Thus Department II capitalists' consumption is $750 - 100 - 50 = 600 = s_{23}$.

Consumption Demand

Demand by workers for consumption goods:

I	$1000v_1 + 100\Delta v_1 =$	1100
II	$750v_2 + 50\Delta v_2 =$	800
Total demand of workers		1900

Demand by capitalists for consumption goods:

I	$500s_{13}$
II	$600s_{23}$
Capitalists' total demand	1100

Aggregate demand for consumption goods = 1900 + 1100 = 3000 = supply of consumption goods by Department II.

I	$4000c_1 \rightarrow 4400c_1$	$1000v_1 \rightarrow 1100v_1$
II	$1500c_2 \rightarrow 1600c_2$	$750v_2 \rightarrow 800v_2$

At the end *of Year '0' (or Beginning of Year '1')*:

	c	v	s	w
I	4400	1100	1100	6600
II	1600	800	800	3200
				9800

At the End of Year 1 (or Beginning of Year 2)

	c	v	s	w
I	4840	1210	1210	7260
II	1760	880	880	3520

etc.

In the first year, Department I grows at 10% while Department II grows at 6.67%. In the second year *both* Departments grow at a balanced rate of 10%. Given the peculiar assumptions made, it is not surprising that the model converges very rapidly to a balanced growth path.

Although *we* can treat this as a two-sector model of balanced growth, Marx considers it to show how even under 'pure' conditions of balanced growth, money and circulation allow for the realisation of surplus value. This surplus value is then used for capital accumulation and hence leads to a growing economy. Let me quote Marx:

The fact that the production of commodities is the general form of capitalist production implies the role which money is playing in it not only as a

> medium of circulation, but also as money-capital, and engenders certain conditions of normal exchange peculiar to this mode of production and therefore of the normal course of reproduction, whether it be on a simple or on an extended scale — conditions which change into so many conditions of abnormal movement, into so many possibilities of crises, *since a balance is itself an accident owing to the spontaneous nature of this production.*
>
> ... *This process is so complicated that it offers ever so many occasions for running abnormally.*
>
> (*KII*, Ch. XXI, p. 495 — emphasis added)

However, if we were to treat this as a model of growth, then there are some worrying features about it. First, the implied investment (accumulation) behaviour is peculiar. Even though the value profit rates differ, capitalists invest only in their *own* Department. This behaviour conflicts with that discussed in *KI*, where competitive behaviour leads to an equalisation of the profit rate. Secondly, why do capitalists maintain a *constant* organic composition of capital? In *KI* Marx argues that capitalist development leads to technological change and an increasing organic composition of capital. Thirdly, why do capitalists of Department II act so obligingly as to maintain equilibrium? Fourthly, why does the rate of profit remain constant over time? This is inconsistent with Marx's arguments in *KIII*. Fifth, why are crises not analysed in the growth context?

All these criticims would be valid if Marx were analysing a growth model. However, as I have stressed before, Marx is *not* concerned with growth as such. He is attempting to show that even assuming the best possible case for bourgeois economics (an equilibrium model of a stationary or growing economy), surplus value is created in production and is realised in exchange (circulation).

8.5 Conclusions

It is worth reminding the reader that Volume II of *Capital* was assembled by Engels from assorted manuscripts at different stages of completion. Had Marx completed *KII*, some of the problems of interpreting it may not have arisen. However, a thorough reading of *KII* shows Marx's concern was with the role of money in a capitalist economy, whether it be a stationary or growing one. He was also at pains to show how capitalists could get more back from a system than they put in it. The surplus value could not be the result of a process of circulation since, in aggregate, one person's gain is another person's loss: it is a zero-sum game. The surplus value is created in production but goes through the circulation process, thus disguising the exploitation from *all* its participants — from the workers and the capitalists.

Marx's analysis of the role of money in a capitalist economy provides several important insights. His analysis of a two sector (Department) model of a growing economy has provided a stimulus to growth models of the von Neumann type. However, these formal growth models tend to underplay (or ignore) the importance of money. A possible development of Marx's ideas would be to study the disequilibrium dynamics when markets do not clear. However, that is an area which is only just being discovered. It is clear that Marx did not believe the capitalist system would grow at a steady state equilibrium rate. His analysis in *KII* simply outlines the several weak links in the chain of circulation which increase the possibility of crises.

Notes to Chapter 8

1. See *KII*, Ch. XVII, p. 328 ff.
2. Note that these assumptions are slightly different from those set out in Chapter 3.
3. See *KII*, Ch. XVII, p. 345.
4. See *KII*, Ch. XXI, p. 501.

Further Reading for Chapter 8

1. *KII*, especially Chs I–IV, XVII, XX and XXI
*2. Desai (1979) Chs V, VI, XIV–XVII
*3. Morishima (1973) Chs 9, 10
4. Sweezy (1942) pp. 75–79 and Ch. 10

Note
*Advanced mathematical reading

... capitalist production moves through certain periodical cycles. It moves through a state of quiescence, growing animation, prosperity, overtrade, crisis and stagnation.
(*Wages, Price and Profit* in *SWI*, p. 440)

9 Crises

9.1 Introduction

Marx's analysis of the cyclical nature of capitalist economies provides penetrating insights for the development of formal models of the trade cycle. Marx does not have any systematic and coherent explanation of cyclical behaviour: the discussion is scattered amidst the three volumes of *Capital* and Part 2 of *Theories of Surplus Value*. However, he pinpoints several elements that have been incorporated in subsequent models of the trade (business) cycle. Crises[1] for Marx are inherent in capitalist economies. Crises lead to a temporary resolution of the contradictions of capitalism and pave the way for its subsequent growth and development. Marx argued that there was a decennial cycle and that the crises would become increasingly severe. Unlike Keynesians who believe cyclical behaviour can be controlled by appropriate government policies, Marx believed that crises were inevitable in a capitalist economy and hence the only way of curing cyclical behaviour was to remove capitalism. It is important to remember that Marx is analysing a system that is in motion as the result of contradictory forces within it.[2] In Marxist language, the forces of production come into conflict with the relations of production, expressing themselves in a crisis.

Before I turn to outlining Marx's theory of crises, let me discuss some preliminary, but fundamental, concepts. It is important to distinguish between (a) factors that allow the *possibility* of crises occurring, (b) factors that *cause* crises, and (c) factors that are the *symptoms* of crises. According to Marx, production for exchange in a capitalist economy where money is both a medium of exchange and a store of value provides for the *possibility* of crises. The proximate *causes* of crises are found in the cyclical nature of the accumulation process. The *symptoms* of crises are the bankruptcies of firms and breakdowns in the credit and monetary system. It is important not to confuse the symptoms with the causes.

There are different levels of explanation of the causes of crises. Firstly, on an *abstract* level the causes of crises are to do with the inner contradictions of capitalism. On a *concrete* level the crises are caused by the instability of accumulation. Later on I shall discuss why accumulation is unstable and how it leads to cyclical behaviour. In explaining crises it is also worth distinguishing between static explanations (e.g. inadequate aggregate demand) and dynamic explanations (e.g. multiplier-accelerator interactions). For the dynamic explanations it is important to distinguish what event *triggers* the crises and the transmission or propagation mechanism of the initial impulse. The initial impulse may be an *exogenous* event like a war or a crop failure, or an *endogenous* event like a fall in the rate of profit.

Although the word crisis means a turning point, Marx discusses the entire trade cycle from boom to slump. A theory of the trade cycle has to explain the following features:

(a) The upswing or boom period.
(b) The upper turning point, the crisis.
(c) The downswing or recession (depression) period.
(d) The lower turning point or revival (recovery).
(e) The period (or length) of the cycle.
(f) The amplitude of the cycle, whether it is constant, increasing or decreasing.

These are illustrated in Diagram 9.1.

Armed with these concepts we are now in a position to analyse various aspects of the trade cycle.

9.2 A Marxian Account of the Trade Cycle

In this section I shall present a synthesised account of the trade cycle. It attempts to integrate various strands of Marx's analysis presented

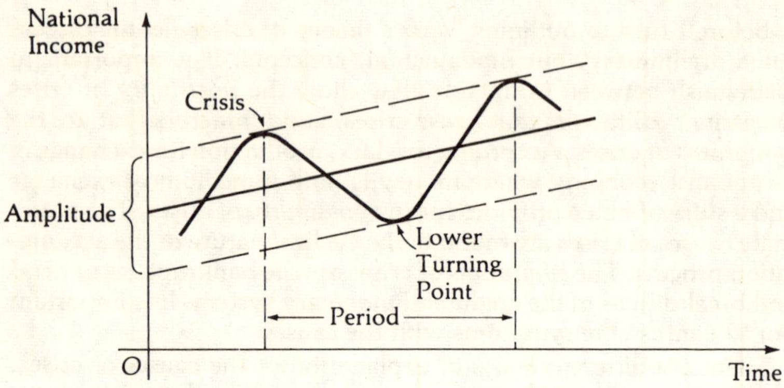

Diagram 9.1 *The Trade Cycle*

by him in different places and at different times. In the subsequent sections I shall attempt to disentangle the conditions that make a crisis possible, by examining its causes and its symptoms. In the process of providing a synthetic account I shall try to stick as closely to Marx as possible, although the presentation and language will, in places, be using some more familiar (and recent) concepts. To avoid breaks in the exposition, in this section I shall not substantiate this interpretation by quotes from Marx. In subsequent sections I shall quote Marx to justify my interpretation. Throughout this chapter, I shall assume, following Marx, that values equal prices. If commodities sell at prices below their values it means that they are selling at disequilibrium prices, below long-run average costs.

Marx's analysis of the trade cycle is set firmly in the context of a mid-nineteenth century European capitalist economy, with Britain as the paradigm. The analysis is therefore of a developed capitalist economy where capitalists produce for profit by exchanging their commodities for money. The capitalists are 'good' capitalists: they aim to maximise profits and to accumulate (invest in constant and variable capital) to increase their capital stock. They buy labour power from a dispossessed proletariat at its value and produce surplus value by exploiting the workers. The capitalists are operating in a competitive system where the benefits of an innovation are temporary, but the lazy capitalist is heading for extinction via bankruptcy or as the prey of a successful capitalist. In this Darwinian struggle of the survival of the fittest, the capitalist is continually accumulating, i.e. innovating and expanding.[3] The capitalist, then, is continually expanding his production of commodities. The aim of the capitalist is to produce for exchange, not for use. Does this continual expansion of exchange value hit against a barrier of inadequate demand? If so, what happens? Before I answer these crucial questions let me turn to emphasising another important aspect of a developed capitalist economy.

In this capitalist economy money plays an important and central role.[4] All commodities (including labour power) have to be exchanged for money. Money is a unique commodity that exchanges for all commodities and is both a medium of exchange and a store of value. Money provides the possibility of moving general purchasing power over time and space. It is possible for a capitalist to sell commodities today in Hampstead and purchase commodities next year in Hull. The producers of commodities in Hull have no way of knowing this potential demand for next year: the hoarding of this unique commodity means that appropriate signals are not transmitted to other capitalists. Marx argues that money simply exposes the contradictions inherent in a commodity. Why do capitalists hoard money? Can this become a general phenomenon with all capitalists selling, but not buying, hoarding money? Again, let me postpone answering the question until a bit later in this section.

Let me now turn to an account of different phases of the cycle. First the upswing or boom period. During the process of capitalist development capitalists accumulate and this leads (via the multiplier) to increasing employment and output. Increasing employment leads to a decrease in the industrial reserve army which increases upward pressure on wages.[5] The increase in wages leads to a (cyclical) fall in the rate of profit (around its presumed downward trend).[6] The increasing accumulation, which incorporates innovations, leads to an obsolescence of existing capital stock, so that capitalists who are slow at the innovation game find they are producing at higher than average costs and making below average profits. The expanding output and sales boost capitalists' expectations about future sales and via the accelerator lead to increased accumulation. Thus the multiplier-accelerator interactions lead to a rapid upswing. However, this upswing eventually comes to an end. The second phase of the cycle, the crisis or upper turning point comes about due to several reasons. (i) As accumulation leads to increased wages and hence a lower rate of profit, after a point the rate of profit falls below a 'normal' level and this leads to a cut-back in accumulation.[7] (ii) The capitalists who are slow at innovating and therefore high cost producers go bankrupt. Because of the financial system these bankruptcies are transmitted to other firms: the bankrupt firms are unable to meet their payments which they had agreed to on the expectation of normal sales. The disruption is amplified by the numerous linkages through the credit system. (iii) The expansion period is one where different sectors (Departments) expand at different rates. Specifically, the capital goods sector expands faster than the consumption goods sector (disproportionality). This uneven growth is not possible for long, since the capital goods sector cannot buy inputs to satisfy its demands. It is therefore forced to slow down production and via the multiplier this leads to a fall in national income. (This could also be treated as a 'ceiling' in a Hicksian multiplier-accelerator model. The ceiling results from a physical full employment level of output.) (iv) Because of over-expansion, capital goods firms cannot sell their output. Because they cannot sell their output, they do not demand inputs, including labour. Because labour is unemployed it does not have an income. Because it does not have an income it does not buy goods. Because of this firms cannot sell consumption goods etc.

The crisis has begun. The third phase of the cycle is the downswing or depression. The multiplier-accelerator now works in reverse. Because output is falling, investment falls which leads to falling output and employment. The IRA increases and hence wages fall and this eventually raises the rate of profit. The smaller capitalists get bankrupted. A 'restructuring' of capital takes place. The bigger capitalist firms buy out machinery from bankrupted capitalists at giveaway prices in the expectation of future good times. Because of an imperfect capital market, the smaller capitalists cannot borrow to wait for the upturn, while the larger capitalists have greater resources and easier access to the capital market. Concentration of firms increases and the way is paved for an eventual upturn.

The final phase of the cycle is the lowering turning point or the revival (recovery) point. The recovery is aided by two factors. First, a replacement investment cycle which follows, Marx argues, a ten-year period. Old capital goods are depreciating and need replacing. This increases the demand for capital goods and marks the end of the depression. Secondly, the restructuring of capital has given the bigger capitalists a chance to expand using capital goods bought at very low prices and hence they can produce at low unit costs. The downswing also puts downward pressure on wages (via the IRA). Together, these help to lead to an upturn in the rate of profit and more optimistic conditions for an expansion. The cycle now repeats itself, although with an increasing amplitude.

Having presented a brief synthetic account of the cycle, I now turn to disentangling various aspects of the cycle in terms of possibility/causes/symptoms.

9.3 Possibility of Crises

The factors that provide the possibility of crisis are: (a) the contradiction between use value and exchange value in a commodity; (b) the existence of money which is a medium of exchange and a store of value; (c) capitalist production for exchange; and (d) the numerous (unplanned) circuits of capital.

In a society based on production for self-consumption, a subsistence economy, there would be production for use, not exchange. There would be good and bad years according to the vagaries of the weather, but no cyclical behaviour would be observed. In an economy which produced commodities for exchange, *but without money*, there would be no possibility of crises. Production of commodities for exchange is at once a demand for other commodities. In a barter economy, Say's Law would rule: supply creates its own demand.

In a capitalist economy with money, capitalists produce commodities for exchange. The existence of money exposes the contradiction between use value and exchange value of a commodity.

> The *most abstract form of crisis* (and therefore the formal possibility of crisis) is thus the *metamorphosis of the commodity* itself; the contradiction of exchange-value and use-value, and furthermore, of money and commodity, exists in metamorphosis only as an involved movement.
>
> (*TSVII*, Ch. XVII, p. 509)

Under capitalist production and exchange ($M - \hat{C} - M'$) there occurs a split between buying and selling.

> But no one is forthwith bound to purchase, because he has just sold. Circulation bursts through all restrictions as to time, place and individuals, imposed by direct barter . . .
>
> (*KI*, Ch. III, p. 113)

> . . . if the split between the sale and the purchase becomes too pronounced, the intimate connection between them, their owners, asserts itself by producing — a crisis.
>
> (*KI*, Ch. III, p. 114)

In Chapter 8 I discussed the circuits of capital which consist of numerous transactions. The possibility of the process of circulation breaking down is greater with the increasing division of labour.[8] The existence of money as a store of value allows for a break between the process of production and circulation.

> The *possibility* of crisis, which became apparent in the *simple metamorphosis* of the commodity, is once more demonstrated, and further developed, by the disjunction between the (direct) process of production and the process of circulation. As soon as these processes do not merge smoothly into one another but become independent of one another, the crisis is there.
>
> (*TSVII*, Ch. XVII, p. 507)

In several places, Marx argues that because a capitalist economy is unplanned, there are several possibilities of a breakdown in the circulation process. Since the circulation process is posited on the production process, the production process is interrupted. An equilibrium is simply a possible balance of contradictory (or opposing) forces, hence the possibility of disequilibrium must be considered as the more likely case.

9.4 Causes of Crises

In the previous section I outlined Marx's discussion of the possibility of crises. That was relatively easy, since he is quite explicit and consistent in his explanation. However, when we turn to discussing the causes of crises Marx's analysis is confusing, if not confused.[9] What I shall do is try to present Marx's arguments as clearly as possible and leave an assessment until the final section. Sweezy (1942) discusses the causes of crises under two headings: (a) Falling rate of profit and (b) Realisation. It seems to me more appropriate to discuss the explanations under the following headings: (i) Abstract causes and (ii) Concrete causes. In the discussion I shall attempt to locate the causes in a particular sphere (or spheres) of production, circulation and distribution. I shall also distinguish between static and dynamic explanations.

(i) *Abstract Causes*

A cause of crises, at an abstract level, is the continual expansion of accumulation in an uncoordinated (unplanned) economy. This accumulation by competitive capitalists takes place on the expectations of future sales to consumers. Since workers are paid their value, which they consume, and they produce surplus value which they cannot purchase even if they produced subsistence commodities, capitalists must somehow consume or accumulate the surplus. If capitalists do not fill the gap between production and workers' consumption, then there is a crisis. Since there is only a long-run tendency for accumulation, this provides only an abstract cause of crises. Marxists argue that the forces of production are being constrained by relations of production developed earlier and a conflict arises which leads to a crisis. The relations of production change to accommodate the changed forces of production.

Another cause of crises, on an abstract level, is due to the falling rate of profit. Again, as we said in Chapter 6, for Marx, this is a long-run tendency. This is an abstract cause of crisis, since capitalist production is for profit. Since the rate of profit has a tendency to fall, there is a threat to accumulation and hence to the capitalist system itself.[10]

> . . . the falling rate of profit [is] a law which at a certain point comes into antagonistic conflict with this development and must be overcome constantly through crises.
>
> (*KIII*, Ch. XV, p. 258)

> From time to time the conflict of antagonistic agencies finds vent in crises. The crises are always but momentary and forcible solutions of the existing contradictions. They are violent eruptions which for a time restore the disturbed equilibrium.
>
> (*KIII*, Ch. XV, p. 249)

Note that both these abstract causes are long-run tendencies in the production sphere and even if we accept the premises, they do not explain why they should result in *cyclical* movements. For that we must turn to the concrete causes.

(ii) *Concrete Causes*

Concrete causes may be located in the production or distribution sphere but have repercussions on the circulation process. It is therefore difficult to isolate concrete causes in any one particular sphere. For purposes of exposition I shall consider concrete causes under two sub-headings: (a) Accumulation problems and (b) Effective Demand problems.

(a) *Accumulation Problems* As outlined in Section 2 above, the trade cycle is explained by Marx in terms of the volatility of accumulation. The trigger mechanism that marks the onset of a crisis is an endogenous fall in the rate of profit below some 'normal' level. This leads to a fall in accumulation which via the circulation process (circuits of capital) leads to a fall in prices and inability to sell commodities. This means capitalists are unable to produce and sell according to their previously expected prices. Various arrangements to buy inputs on credit can no longer be met and debts cannot be paid, thus leading to bankruptcies. Incomes fall, consumption falls, therefore production falls, etc. This amplifying process is the familiar Keynesian multiplier process. As discussed earlier, this also leads to a fall in accumulation via the accelerator, a fall in income, etc.

What is the cause of the crisis? Is it the fall in the rate of profit? Or the fall in accumulation? What made the rate of profit fall below 'normal'? If it is the long-run fall in the rate of profit, why should capitalists follow this cyclical path for accumulation? It is possible to argue that the long-term fall in the rate of profit is seen by some individual capitalists as a fall in *their* rate of profit, so they respond by a cut-back in accumulation. Given that Marx is analysing an economy with capitalists possessing different vintages of capital stock, some are more efficient than others. Even if the average rate of profit falls, some capitalists manage to do well. However, it needs only *some* capitalists to cut back accumulation for this to lead to a cumulative fall in accumulation via the multiplier-accelerator interactions. In this argument, the concrete form of crisis is related to an abstract cause.

A more plausible line of argument is that the endogenous fall in the rate of profit is due to an increase in wages, which is due to a fall in the IRA which in turn is due to an increase in accumulation. This line of argument is that the concrete cause of crisis is to be found in the cyclical nature of the rate of profit, wages and accumulation.

Another cause of crises related to accumulation problems is due to the discontinuous nature of technical change and innovations. A sudden increase in innovations by some capitalists makes the capital owned by other capitalists obsolescent. This 'disturbs the given conditions, within which the process of circulation and reproduction of capital takes place and is therefore accompanied by sudden stoppages and crises in the production process' (*KIII*, Ch. XV, p. 249). The trigger mechanism here is the sudden changes in innovations. The propagation mechanism is the circuits of capital which are based on production and reproduction.

Another cause of crises related to accumulation is due to the disproportional growth of different Departments. By Marx's analysis, the capital goods Department (sector) expands more rapidly than the other Departments. This leads to a crisis because eventually physical limits are reached and the capital goods sector is unable to buy inputs to satisfy its demands.[11] As soon as it is forced to slow down accumulation, it leads, via the circuits of capital, to an amplification of the disturbance.

At one place Marx even allows for a random exogenous event, a crop failure due to bad weather, to lead to a crisis. A crop failure raises the costs of inputs of (say) the textile industry, hence leaving less money capital available for hiring labour. Reproduction cannot be continued on a previously established scale. Workers are unemployed, they have less incomes, less consumption, etc. Again the initial disturbance is amplified via the circuits of capital.[12]

All the above causes of crises are explanations of the upper turning point. The lower turning point is explained in terms of a replacement cycle for capital goods (echo effects) and an eventual rise in the rate of profit due to a decrease in unit costs of production via lower wages and cheaper second hand capital bought from bankrupt capitalists.

(b) *Effective Demand Problems* Marx sometimes explains the crises in terms of effective demand problems (realisation problems). However, this is essentially a static explanation of unemployment, rather than a dynamic explanation of the trade cycle. What makes it particularly difficult to outline Marx's arguments on realisation problems is that he makes statements that are in direct contradiction to each other.

Marx's arguments against Say's Law are powerful and anticipate Keynes' attack on the Classical school.

> At a given moment, the supply of all commodities can be greater than the demand for all commodities, since the demand for the *general commodity*, money, exchange-value, is greater than the demand for all particular commodities, in other words the motive to turn the commodity into money, to realise its exchange value, prevails over the motive to transform the commodity again into use-value.
>
> (*TSVII*, Ch. XVII, p. 505)

To put it differently, there is inadequate demand for commodities because people hoard money for future purchases. There is a passage in one of Marx's early writings on economics, which is a clear anticipation of Clower's dual decision hypothesis, or income constrained behaviour.[13]

> In all crises the following circular movement relates to the workers:
>
> The employer cannot employ the workers because he cannot sell his product. He cannot sell his product because he has no buyers. He has no buyers because the workers have nothing to offer in exchange but their labour and precisely for that reason they cannot exchange their labour.
>
> (*Wages*, 1847, in *CW* Vol. 6, pp. 424–5)

As mentioned earlier, Marx often argues that capitalists expand production continually, but may be unable to realise the surplus value produced because aggregate demand is inadequate, i.e. that the 'market expands more slowly than production' (*TSVII*, Ch. XVII, p. 524). Marx argues that capitalists continually expand production, but the distribution of income is such that there would be underconsumption.

> But the more productiveness develops, the more it finds itself at variance with the narrow basis on which the conditions of consumption rest.
>
> (*KIII*, Ch. XV, p. 245)

and

> The ultimate reason for all real crises always remains the poverty and restricted consumption of the masses as opposed to the drive of capitalist production to develop the productive forces as though only the absolute consuming power of society constituted their limit.
>
> (*KIII*, Ch. XV, p. 484)

However, in *KII*, Marx argues categorically that crises are not caused by inadequate demand.

> It is sheer tautology to say that crises are caused by the scarcity of effective consumption, or of effective consumers. The capitalist system does not know any other modes of consumption than effective ones, ... But if one were to attempt to give this tautology the semblance of a profounder justification by saying that the working-class receives too small a portion of its own product and the evil would be remedied as soon as it receives a larger share of it and its wages increase in consequence, one could only remark that crises are always prepared by precisely a period in which wages rise generally and the working-class actually gets a larger share of that part of the annual product which is intended for consumption. From the point of view of these advocates of sound and 'simple'(!) common sense, such a period should rather remove the crisis. It appears, then, that capitalist production comprises conditions independent of good or bad will, conditions which permit the working-class to enjoy that relative prosperity only momentarily, and at that always only as the harbinger of a coming crisis.
>
> (*KII*, Ch. XX, pp. 410–11)

A possible resolution of those conflicting statements is that during a crisis there is over-production or under-consumption. This is only a symptom of the crisis. The cause of the crisis is to be found elsewhere. At an abstract level it is still Marx's view that the possibility of crises is due to the inherent nature of a capitalist system: a capitalist employs labour power at its value and creates surplus value. Unless there is a capitalist demand for this surplus value, there is the possibility of a crisis. Over time capitalists increase surplus value; therefore they must continually increase their demand for the surplus value, either for consumption purposes or for accumulation. Hence the view that there is a constant tendency for over-production.

It is clear that even if we accept that over-production or under-consumption occurs, it only explains, in a static sense, the level of unemployment. It does not explain the cyclical behaviour of the economic aggregates.

9.5 Symptoms of Crises

As mentioned in the previous section, over-production may be considered simply as a symptom of crisis rather than its cause. Immediately prior to a crisis (the upper turning point), Marx argues that prices are rising, business looks healthy[14] and wages are beginning to increase. Because business is healthy, capitalists are keen to borrow money capital for productive purposes, so that there is shortage of money capital and interest rates are high. Immediately after a crisis wages fall, there is a surplus of loanable capital and business is in disarray. The entire monetary and credit system comes under strain.

> . . . definite, presupposed, price relations govern the process of reproduction, so that the latter is halted and thrown into confusion by a general drop in prices. This confusion and stagnation paralyses the function of money as a medium of payment, whose development is geared to the development of capital and is based on those presupposed price relations. The chain of payment obligations due at specific dates is broken in a hundred places. The confusion is augmented by the attendant collapse of the credit system, which develops simultaneously with capital, and leads to violent and acute crises, to sudden and forcible depreciations, to the actual stagnation and disruption of the process of reproduction and thus to a real falling off in reproduction.
>
> (*KIII*, Ch. XV, p. 254)

For Marx then, changes in money supply or interest rates are simply symptoms of the crises not their cause. Similarly, bankruptcies are symptoms of crises, not their causes. Of course, bankruptcies lead to an amplified disturbance in the circuits of capital and hence a prolonged depression. The re-structuring of capital that takes place (the increased concentration and buying of second-hand capital goods from bankrupted capitalists) provides for the recovery.

9.6 Conclusions

So far I have given an account of Marx's explanation of the possibility, causes and symptoms of crises. Because of the scattered and incomplete nature of this aspect of Marx's work, it is difficult to give a clear and consistent account. I have attempted to provide an account which is in sympathy with Marx's writings, although at times I have had to go beyond interpreting Marx. On an abstract level, according to Marx, the causes of crises are contained in capitalism itself. On a concrete level, crises are caused by events in the production sphere that have repercussions on the circulation and distribution spheres. Because of the interdependent nature of the analysis, it is difficult to pinpoint *the* cause of crises.

In assessing Marx's analysis of crises, let me evaluate it under three headings. First, to what extent does Marx succeed in explaining the different aspects of crises? Secondly, does the empirical evidence support Marx's analysis? Finally, what is Marx's contribution to the economic analysis of the trade cycle?

In Section 9.1 I set out the different features of the cycle that need to be explained. To what extent does Marx's analysis explain the different features? The upswing is explained, in effect, in terms of a multiplier-accelerator relationship. Capital accumulation is the driving force. This aspect is accepted by most Keynesians and seems well-founded. The upper turning point or crisis is explained by a fall in accumulation when the rate of profit falls below a normal level. This analysis needs some strengthening. What determines the 'normal' rate of profit? Why should accumulation fall rather than just continue increasing at a slower rate? Perhaps the idea of a ceiling is a better explanation: output expands less rapidly, hence a fall in accumulation via the accelerator relationship. As discussed earlier, one of Marx's explanations is in terms of competitive capitalists, where the actions of some capitalists in slowing down have negative feedback effects via the circuits of capital. Clearly, there are the elements of an explanation, even if it is not formally presented. The downswing is explained in terms of multiplier-accelerator interaction. Again this seems acceptable to most Keynesians. The next sticky point is the lower turning point. Here Marx's explanation is in terms of a replacement cycle and the purchase of cheap second-hand capital goods in the expectation of future good times. The latter appears a 'bootstrap' explanation: expectations of good times lead to good times. This may, of course, be what happens in the real world. For replacement to lead to a recovery we would need a bunching of replacement investment which, in a diversified economy, is unlikely. Overall, it is instability of accumulation in a capitalist economy which leads to cyclical behaviour. Marx further argued that the cycles would increase in severity. There is little analytical justification for this view, other than the increasing complexity of the circuits of capital.

What empirical evidence is there for cyclical behaviour? Most capitalist economies exhibit a pattern of cyclical behaviour, although there is no evidence of an increasing amplitude in the cycle. There is a fair bit of evidence to support a modified accelerator theory of investment and multiplier effects of changes in investment. It is difficult to pinpoint the proximate cause of the upper turning point, or the lower turning point. A fall in the rate of profit seems to coincide with the present crisis in Western capitalist economies, although it would be rash to argue a cause and effect relationship. Clearly, expectations are very important in explaining sudden changes in accumulation behaviour. However, there are few good explanations about the formation of expectations.

It is easy to criticise Marx's theory of crises, since it was not presented in a completed form. I have tried to present a more-or-less consistent account. As I mentioned earlier, it is difficult to obtain cyclical behaviour out of a long-run falling rate of profit. Similarly, it is difficult to obtain cyclical behaviour from under-consumptionist arguments. There is generally little evidence to support Marx's view that, in a recession, (real) wages fall. There is little evidence to support echo effects in replacement investment. However, as I shall argue in the next paragraph, these are minor blemishes when treated in perspective.

Marx's analysis of crises provides an important contribution to an understanding of cyclical behaviour. It was one of the earliest attempts at explaining the cyclical behaviour of capitalist economies. It contains several important elements that were later incorporated into theories of the trade cycle (although often in ignorance of Marx's contribution). Marx clearly distinguishes between the possibility, causes and symptoms of crises, for which he receives an accolade from Schumpeter. His analysis of the role of money and the circuits of capital in amplifying disturbances in many ways anticipates Keynes and subsequent writers. His emphasis on the instability of accumulation as a force that generates cycles is clearly important. Subsequent work by Hicks (1950) formalises the multiplier-accelerator cycle model. Morishima (1973) shows how cyclical behaviour can be obtained in a model of extended reproduction, assuming given propensities to save and invest in two Departments. Goodwin (1967) provides an interesting formal model of the cycle which is the resultant of a class conflict over wages and profits.

Given that capitalism exhibits cyclical properties, why does not the 'executive committee of the bourgeoisie' (the State) control the economy to dampen cycles? Kalecki (1943) has an interesting paper where he argues that, if the economy were continually run at full employment, the workers would begin to get too demanding. A depression would have to be created to teach the workers to accept their (servile) position in a capitalist society. (This is a 'free' interpretation of Kalecki's paper.) Orthodox Marxists argue that the

Government cannot maintain full employment because of the inherent instability of a capitalist economy.

Let me conclude: Marx has made an important contribution to our understanding of trade cycles. However, a lot more work needs to be done to provide a complete and consistent theory that takes account of the relations between the production, circulation and distribution spheres.

Notes to Chapter 9

1. The *Concise Oxford Dictionary* defines crisis as 'Turning point, especially of disease; time of danger or suspense in politics, commerce, etc.'
2. See Chapter 1.
3. See Chapter 4.
4. See Chapter 7.
5. See Chapter 5.
6. See Chapter 6.
7. See Chapter 4.
8. See the quotation from *KII*, Ch. XXI, p. 495 in Section 8.4 referring to the possibility of circuits of capital breaking down.
9. There are philosophical problems involved in determining what is a cause and what is an effect. I shall assume these away.
10. See *KIII*, Ch. XV, pp. 241–2 and 258–9.
11. See Morishima (1973) where he obtains an explosive model by adapting Marx's model of extended reproduction. Cycles can be obtained by imposing floors and ceilings. Also see Desai (1973).
12. See *TSVII*, Ch. XVII, pp. 515–6.
13. Also see *TSVII*, Ch. XVII, pp. 522–3.
14. See *KIII*, Ch. XXX, pp. 484–5, 490–1.

Further Reading for Chapter 9

1. *KIII* Chs 15, 30
2. *TSVII* Ch. XVII (especially pp. 492–535)
3. *Grundrisse* pp. 410–24
4. Sweezy (1942) Chs 8–10
5. Itoh (1980) Chs 4, 5
6. Shoul (1957)
7. Weisskopf (1979)
8. Hicks (1950) especially Ch. 8
9. Matthews (1959) especially Ch. 2
10. Goodwin (1967)
11. Kalecki (1943)

Concern for man himself and his fate must always form the chief interest for all technical endeavours . . . Never forget this in the midst of your diagrams and equations.

(Albert Einstein)

10 Conclusions

10.1 Preliminaries

In this book I have attempted to provide a more-or-less consistent account of Marx's economics. At times, interpretation may have verged on invention but, on the whole, the discussion sticks fairly closely to Marx's writing. By all accounts he was an extraordinary man. His multi-faceted study of society has several gems of wisdom. However, his main contribution lies in an analytical method which studies society as a unified whole. He combined an ability to carry out abstract analysis with an ability to use historical information which is unrivalled then and now. *Capital* oscillates between very high levels of abstraction and minute details on, for example, wages for agricultural labour in villages in Essex. Even if particular aspects of his analysis have been superseded by modern research, his general method is a powerful tool. By his own analysis, if there have been significant changes in the economic structure, then various relationships would also change. Hence the details of Marx's analysis would have to be altered, but the method of analysis would remain.

In previous chapters I have outlined Marx's theories and discussed some of the criticisms levelled at them. In general, evaluating an outstanding figure in the history of economic thought is difficult. For better or worse there is a natural instinct to interpret past work using our existing knowledge and paradigms: there is a danger of reading too much into past work. How should we, then, evaluate an economist from the past? Should we compare him with other economists of his day? Or should we compare him with present-day economists? Should we 'simply' assess the scientific status of his theory? Because of the revolutionary implications of Marx's analysis it is difficult to find many dispassionate evaluations of his work: on the one hand there are dogmatic supporters and on the other, the rabid anti-Marxists. It is important, nonetheless, to separate out Marx's work from the benefits or evils of the socialist or communist states of the world. Marx's analysis was, after all, almost entirely an analysis of *capitalist* states. An assessment of Marx must, therefore, be independent of one's feelings towards Hungary or Czechoslovakia, Poland or Afghanistan, Stalin or Mao.

Let me outline the remainder of this chapter. Section 2 highlights the key elements of Marx's economics, Section 3 evaluates Marx's contribution to economic theory and the validity of his predictions. Section 4 discusses some extensions to Marx's theory and Section 5 concludes the chapter.

10.2 Key Elements in Marx's Economics

To appreciate Marx's economic analysis, we have to understand the underlying philosophical basis of historical materialism. Marx is analysing a society in motion: the motion is the resultant of its inner contradictions. A capitalist society consists of two opposing classes: the capitalists and the workers. The mode of production determines the relations of production: hence if you want to change the relations of production you must change the mode of production. Cosmetic changes in distributional relations will not remove the conflicts in society. An analysis of the 'laws of motion' of a capitalist society must therefore begin with an analysis of production, even though production, circulation and distribution are interdependent. Hence, the emphasis in Volume I of *Capital* on production.

To understand Marx's economics we must understand the labour theory of value. For Marx, surplus value is created in the production sphere, not in the process of circulation. The concept of exploitation, the appropriation of surplus value by the capitalist, is central to Marx's economics. Marx provides a powerful result when he shows that exploitation takes place *even under competitive conditions*. This is what Morishima refers to as Marx's 'fundamental theorem'.

Exploitation, for Marx, is therefore not an accidental result of cheating or monopoly power, but the necessary result of a competitive system. This has important political and social implications: hence the controversy over Marx's labour theory of value. The realisation of this surplus value takes place in the process of circulation and leads to the famous transformation problem. Even that problem is treated by Marx independently of demand conditions, implicitly because of his assumption of constant returns to scale. The role of money in facilitating the realisation of surplus value is discussed in Volume II of *Capital*.

The central role of production is emphasised by Marx's analysis of the falling rate of profit. Problems of inadequate aggregate demand are not raised in the discussion. The law of the tendency of the rate of profit to fall is explained in terms of increasing organic composition of capital as a result of labour saving capital accumulation. Capital accumulation also leads to an increasing industrial reserve army. Crises are explained, on an abstract level, by the falling rate of profit and the internal contradictions of capitalism. The causes of crises, on a concrete level, are due to an interaction of the circulation, production and distribution spheres. The distribution of income is determined as a result of the production process and the relative strengths of workers and capitalists.

10.3 Marx's Contribution to Economics

First let me outline Marx's contribution to economic theory and then return to an evaluation of the theory and some of his predictions. Although, Marx was (and is) ignored by bourgeois economists, he made several important contributions which would be accepted by some of them now. First, Marx's analysis was of a general equilibrium nature and studied the interactions between different sectors. General equilibrium ideas had been around since Adam Smith and the Physiocrats. However, Marx's numerical examples of models of simple reproduction give a greater precision to them. Marx's analysis of the role of money in a general equilibrium framework is a perceptive, though incomplete, account. Marx's analysis of models of reproduction provides an excellent basis for input—output models of growing economies. In some ways they are a precursor of von Neumann models. Marx's analysis of capital accumulation has several elements that a Keynesian would quite happily accept. His analysis of crises (again incomplete) has several features (e.g. the multiplier-accelerator and the role of money as a store of value) which are now familiar to traditional economists. His emphasis on the role of capital accumulation in determining employment and fluctuations in employment, is again something which Keynesians would accept. Morishima (1974) argues that Marx was an important mathematical economist, although he used virtually no mathematics. However, he posed important problems that mathematical economists solved subsequently. Overall, even a traditional (bourgeois) economist could learn a lot by reading Marx, even if he ignored Marx's philosophical approach. To summarise, Marx made some important contributions to economic theory. However, since he was neglected, many of his contributions were not developed subsequently. An historian of economic thought has to reject Samuelson's snide remark that Marx was a 'minor post-Ricardian'!

Let me turn to some of Marx's predictions. Marx predicted that in the process of capitalist development, there would be increasing concentration of capital, a falling rate of profit, an increasing industrial reserve army and recurring crises.[1] In previous chapters I argued that there was some evidence to support Marx's prediction of increasing concentration. There is little evidence for a long-term downward trend in the rate of profit, although the evidence of the last decade confirms his prediction. Whether this fall is simply part of a cyclical downturn or a long-term trend can only be judged in time. Again, there has been little evidence to support the prediction of an increasing industrial reserve army. However, the recent crisis in Western capitalist countries has been the most severe and prolonged since the 1930s. In Britain, unemployment has almost reached three million (November 1981) and is forecast to continue increasing (or by some to remain more-or-less constant) for some time to come. Is this a trend? Again, Marx's predictions of the cyclical nature of capitalist economies have been validated by events. Besides the cataclysmic events of the thirties (and now?) the capitalist economies have suffered from minor recessions and booms throughout the past century. The post-war optimism of the Keynesians that they could control the economy has now been replaced by the Monetarists' incantations about the impotence of Government economic policies. The Monetarists and Marxists are strange bed-fellows in arguing that the Government cannot control the fluctuations of a free-enterprise economy! But, of course, for Monetarists the system is inherently stable while, for Marxists, the system is inherently unstable. For Marxists, only a removal of capitalism will remove the cyclical instability.

To summarise, there is some evidence to support some of Marx's predictions. However, Marx's predictions are not usually formulated in a simple testable form. Formal tests of the predictions are not easy and so I have discussed only some casual evidence. Although it would be interesting, I have not discussed Marx's predictions on revolution and socialism.

10.4 Some Extensions to Marx's Economic Theory?

In the discussion so far I have been defensive of Marx's propositions. However, there are several aspects of Marx's work which need extending, using his own methodology. Clearly, since Marx was writing in the 1860s, his analysis is of a capitalist state in its 'middle years'. By his own analysis the capitalist state would change as a result of its own contradictory forces. The development of capitalism over the past hundred years has changed the structure of the economy. Hence we must extend Marx's theory to take account of these new features.[2]

The first major shortcoming of Marx's analysis is the almost complete neglect of international economic relations. In the grand plan a volume was to be devoted to it, but it never appeared. Except for scattered remarks about international trade, there is a vacuum. In recent years, following Baran, writers like Samir Amin and Arghiri Emmanuel have argued that trade between Western capitalist countries and Third World countries has led to an under-development of the Third World. This thesis is an extension of Marx's impoverishment of the working class: the Third World workers are treated as an exploitable mass. Much needs to be done in analysing trade between Western capitalist and Third World countries, as well as between capitalist countries themselves. The rise of multinational enterprises is another feature that needs to be integrated into a Marxian theory of capital accumulation.

A second major shortcoming of Marx's analysis is that he assumes a competitive model. By his own analysis the forces of capital accumulation lead to increasing concentration and hence a breakdown of his model. It is, of course, very difficult to build an abstract model which consists of a few large capitalist firms with international branches. Similarly, the forces of accumulation have led to a dialectical response of increasing unionisation of workers. This increases the complexity of the analysis. A beginning has been made in Baran and Sweezy's *Monopoly Capital* (1966) and in Mandel's *Late Capitalism* (1975). However, there is no powerful analytical structure comparable with Marx's model.

A third major shortcoming of Marx's analysis for today's world is the absence of an analysis of the role of the State in a world of monopoly capitalism. The State taxes, subsidises and spends money directly on health, education, transport and defence (to name just a few expenditures). How does this affect capital accumulation, the rate of profit, unemployment, distribution of income, etc? The debate is lively and is reviewed in Fine and Harris (1979). Another major shortcoming in Marx's analysis is the lack of a theory of inflation.

Several Marxists are actively engaged in attempting to solve these important problems. The interested reader should turn to the references at the end of this chapter.

10.5 A Final Word

In this book I have emphasised Marx's economics. A proper evaluation of Marx's contribution must also include his contributions to historical analysis, sociological analysis and political analysis. There are few figures in history who have made important contributions to so many fields. In these days when new neo-Classical economists are hiding behind the cloak of 'rational expectations', it is only a question of time before people see through the 'Emperor's new clothes' to expose the emptiness of much of traditional economic theory. Some Marxist economists are busy mathematising Marx, but in the process seem to lose the broad historical 'vision' which was a powerful tool for Marx. Eventually, Marx was interested in making life better for the ordinary working person. His academic work was combined with his political activity in attempting to improve the conditions of mankind. In much of traditional (bourgeois) economics, men and women disappear and are replaced by anonymous 'agents' without any history or power. Political scientists playing games (in both senses) with nuclear weapons may 'rationally' lead to the end of life on earth. In all analyses of society we must not forget our 'concern for man . . .'

Notes to Chapter 10

1. This is not the place to discuss the problems of methodology. Blaug (1980) argues that Marx's predictions are unfalsifiable and, in any case, (he argues) derived from an inconsistent theory. I have argued in the previous chapters that a sympathetic reading of Marx provides a consistent model. Testing of predictions, whether Marxist or neo-Classical, is not an easy matter. If Marxists have what Blaug (following Popper) calls 'immunising stratagems', then bourgeois economists are also surprisingly adept at ignoring or explaining away refutations of their theories. Neo-Classical theories happily predict that (involuntary) unemployment cannot exist in the face of millions of unemployed workers in Western Europe!

2. See Fine and Harris (1979) for a review of some recent debates. A comprehensive discussion of these issues would require another book!

Further Reading for Chapter 10

1. Fine and Harris (1979) Chs 6–10
2. Baran and Sweezy (1966)
3. Baran (1957)
4. Mandel (1975)
5. Amin (1976)
6. Emmanuel (1972)
7. Morishima (1974a)
8. Blaug (1980)

Bibliography

Biographies

Berlin, I. (1963) *Karl Marx*, Oxford University Press, Oxford.
Liebknecht, W. (1975) *Karl Marx: Bibliographical Memoirs*, The Journeyman Press, London.
McLellan, D. (1977) *Engels*, Fontana Books, London.
McLellan, D. (1973) *Karl Marx: His Life and Thought*, Paladin Books, St Albans.
Mehring, R. (1962) *Karl Marx*, Ann Arbor, University of Michigan.
Nicolaievsky, B. & Maenchen-Helfen, O. (1976) *Karl Marx: Man & Fighter*, Penguin Books, Harmondsworth.
Riazanov, D. (1973) *Karl Marx and Friedrich Engels*, Monthly Review Press, New York.

Works by Marx and Engels

Engels, Friedrich (Ms 1843) *Outlines of a Critique of Political Economy*. Reprinted in Marx & Engels, *Collected Works op. cit.*, Vol. 3.
Marx, Karl (Ms 1844) *Economic & Philosophic Manuscripts of 1844*, in Marx & Engels, *Collected Works op. cit.*, Vol. 3.
Marx, Karl (Ms 1847) *Poverty of Philosophy*. Reprinted in Marx & Engels, *Collected Works op. cit.*, Vol. 6.

Marx, Karl (Ms 1847) *Wage, Labour and Capital.* Reprinted in Marx & Engels, *Selected Works op. cit.*, Vol. I.

Marx, Karl (Ms 1857—58) *Grundrisse*, Penguin Books, Harmondsworth & Random House, New York, 1973.

Marx, Karl (Ms 1859) *A Contribution to the Critique of Political Economy*, Progress Publishers, Moscow, 1970.

Marx, Karl (Mss 1862—63) *Theories of Surplus Value*, Parts I—III, Progress Publishers, Moscow, 1963. (First published 1905—10.)

Marx, Karl (Ms 1865) *Wages, Price and Profit.* Reprinted in Marx & Engels, *Selected Works op cit.*, Vol. I.

Marx, Karl (1977) *Capital*, Vols I, II, III, Lawrence & Wishart, London. (First published, Vol. I 1867, Vol. II 1885, Vol. III 1894.)

Marx, Karl & Engels, Friedrich, (1962) *Selected Works*, Vols I & II, Lawrence & Wishart, London.

Marx, Karl & Engels, Friedrich (1975) *Selected Correspondence*, 3rd edn, Progress Publishers, Moscow.

Marx, Karl & Engels, Friedrich (1975—) *Collected Works*, Vols 1— , Lawrence & Wishart, London.

References

Aaronovitch, S. & Sawyer, M.C. (1975) *Big Business: Theoretical & Empirical Aspects of Concentration and Mergers in the UK*, Macmillan, London.

Aaronovitch, S. & Smith, R. (1981) *The Political Economy of British Capitalism*, McGraw-Hill, London.

Amin, S. (1976) *Unequal Development*, Monthly Review Press, New York.

Armstrong, P., Glyn, A. & Harrison, J. (1978) 'In defence of value — a reply to Ian Steedman', *Capital & Class*, Summer, No. 5, pp. 1—31.

Balibar, Etienne (1978) 'Irrationalism & Marxism', *New Left Review*, No. 107, Jan.—Feb., pp. 3—18.

Bank of England (1977) 'Industrial & commercial companies: profitability and the cost of capital', *Bank of England Quarterly Bulletin*, Vol. 17, No. 2, June, pp. 156—61.

Baran, P.A. (1957) *The Political Economy of Growth*, Monthly Review Press, New York.

Baran, P.A. & Sweezy, P.M. (1966) *Monopoly Capital*, Penguin Books, Harmondsworth.

Baumol, W.J. (1959) *Business Behaviour, Value and Growth*, Macmillan, New York.

Baumol, W.J. (1974) 'The transformation of values: what Marx "really" meant', *Journal of Economic Literature*, Vol. XII, No. 1, March, pp. 51—62.

Baumol, W.J. (1976) 'Review of Maarek's *Introduction au capital de Karl Marx*', *Journal of Economic Literature*, Vol. XIV, No. 1, March, pp. 82—7.

Becker, J.F. (1977) *Marxian Political Economy, An Outline*, Cambridge University Press, Cambridge.

Blackburn, R. (ed.) (1972) *Ideology in Social Science*, Fontana Books, London.

Blaug, M. (1978) *Economic Theory in Retrospect*, 3rd edn, Cambridge University Press, Cambridge.

Blaug, M. (1980) *A Methodological Appraisal of Marxian Economics*, de Vries Lectures in Economics, No. 3, North-Holland Publishing Co., Amsterdam.

Bleaney, M. (1976) *Underconsumption Theories*, Lawrence & Wishart, London.

Bliss, C.J. (1975) *Capital Theory & the Distribution of Income*, North-Holland Publishing Co., Amsterdam.

Bortkiewicz, L. von (1906—7) 'On the correction of Marx's fundamental theoretical construction in the third volume of *Capital*', in Sweezy (1973b) *op. cit.*.

Bortkiewicz, L. von (1907) 'Value and price in the Marxian system', translated and reprinted in *International Economic Papers*, No. 2, 1951—52, pp. 5—60.

Bose, A. (1975) *Marxian and Post Marxian Political Economy*, Penguin Books, Harmondsworth.

Bottomore, T. & Rubel, M. (1963) *Karl Marx: Selected Writings in Sociology and Social Philosophy*, Penguin Books, Harmondsworth.

Bradley, I. & Howard, M.C. (eds) (1981) *Classical & Marxian Political Economy*, Macmillan, London.

Braverman, H. (1974) *Labor & Monopoly Capital*, Monthly Review Press, New York.

Brenner, R. (1977) 'The origins of capitalist development: a critique of neo-Smithian Marxism', *New Left Review*, No. 104, July—Aug., pp. 25—92.

Brenner, R. (1978) 'Dobb on the transition from feudalism to capitalism', *Cambridge Journal of Economics*, Vol. 2, No. 2, June, pp. 121—40.

Burmeister, E. (1980) *Capital Theory and Dynamics*, Cambridge University Press, Cambridge.

Clark, T.A. & Williams, N.P. (1978) 'Measures of real profitability', *Bank of England Quarterly Bulletin*, Vol. 18, No. 4, Dec., pp. 513—22.

Clower, R.W. (1969) 'Foundations of monetary theory' in R.W. Clower (ed.) *Monetary Theory: Selected Readings*, Penguin Books, Harmondsworth.

Cogoy, M. (1973) 'The fall of the rate of profit and the theory of accumulation: a reply to Paul Sweezy', *Conference of Socialist Economists Bulletin*, Vol. II.7, Winter, pp. 52—67.

Cornforth, Maurice (1977a) *Materialism & the Dialectical Method*, Lawrence & Wishart, London.

Cornforth, Maurice (1977b) *Historical Materialism*, Lawrence & Wishart, London.

de Brunhoff, Suzanne (1973) *Marx on Money*, Urizen Books, New York.

Desai, M. (1973) 'Growth cycles and inflation in a model of the class struggle', *Journal of Economic Theory*, Vol. 6, pp. 527—45.

Desai, M. (1979) *Marxian Economics*, Basil Blackwell, Oxford.

Dickinson, H.D. (1957) 'The falling rate of profit in Marxian economics', *Review of Economic Studies*, Vol. XXIV(2), No. 64, Feb., pp. 120—30.

Dobb, M. (1963) *Studies in the Development of Capitalism*, Routledge & Kegan Paul, London.

Dobb, M. (1973) *Theories of Value and Distribution since Adam Smith*, Cambridge University Press, Cambridge.

Eatwell, J. (1974) 'Controversies in the theory of surplus value: old and new', *Science and Society*, Vol. 38, No. 3, Fall, pp 281—303.

Emmanuel, A. (1972) *Unequal Exchange: A Study of the Imperialism of Trade*, Monthly Review Press, New York.

Ergas, H. & Fishman, D. (1975) 'The Marxian theory of money and the crisis of capital', *Conference of Socialist Economists Bulletin*, Vol IV.2, No. 11, June, pp. 1—15.

Feldstein, M. & Summers, L. (1977) 'Is the rate of profit falling?', *Brookings Papers on Economic Activity*, Vol. 1, pp. 211—27.

Fine, B. (1975) *Marx's Capital*, Macmillan, London.

Fine, B. & Harris, L. (1976) 'Controversial issues in Marxist economic theory', in R. Miliband & J. Saville (eds), *Socialist Register*, Merlin Press, London.

Fine, B. & Harris, L. (1979) *Rereading Capital*, Macmillan, London.

Flemming, J.S. *et al.* (1976a) 'Trends in company profitability', *Bank of England Quarterly Bulletin*, Vol. 16, No. 1, March, pp. 36—52.

Flemming, J.S. *et al.* (1976b) 'The cost of capital, finance and investment', *Bank of England Quarterly Bulletin*, Vol. 16, No. 2, June, pp. 193—205.

Foley, D.K. (1975) 'Towards a Marxist theory of money', Stanford Institute for Mathematical Studies in the Social Sciences, *Technical Report*, No. 181, September.

Foster-Carter, Aidan (1978) 'The modes of production controversy', *New Left Review*, No. 107, Jan.—Feb., pp. 47—77.

Freedman, R. (ed.) (1962) *Marx on Economics*, Penguin Books, Harmondsworth.

Gamble, A. & Walton, P. (1976) *Capitalism in Crisis*, Macmillan, London.

Gardiner, Jean, Himmelweit, Susan & Mackintosh, Mary (1975) 'Women's domestic labour', *Conference of Socialist Economists Bulletin*, Vol. IV.2, No. 11, June.

Garegnani, P. (1978) 'Sraffa's revival of Marxist economic theory', *New Left Review*, No. 107, Nov.—Dec., pp. 71—3.

Gerstein, I. (1976) 'Production, circulation and value: the significance of the 'transformation problem' in Marx's *Critique of Political Economy*', *Economy & Society*, Vol. V, No. 3, August, pp. 243—9.

Gillman, J. (1957) *The Falling Rate of Profit*, Dobson, London.

Glyn, A. & Harrison, J. (1980) *The British Economic Disaster*, Pluto Press, London.

Glyn, A. & Sutcliffe, B. (1972) *British Capitalism, Workers and the Profits Squeeze*, Penguin Books, Harmondsworth.

Goldthorpe, J.H. *et al.* (1980) *Social Mobility & Class Structure in Modern Britain*, Oxford University Press, Oxford.

Goodwin, R.M. (1967) 'A growth cycle', in C.H. Feinstein (ed.), *Capitalism and Economic Growth*, Cambridge University Press, Cambridge, Reprinted in Hunt & Schwartz (1972) *op. cit.*.

Gorz, A. (ed.) (1978) *The Division of Labour*, Harvester Press, Brighton.

Gough, I. (1972) 'Marx's theory of productive and unproductive labour', *New Left Review*, No. 76, pp. 47—72.

Green, F. & Nore, P. (eds) (1977) *Economics: An Anti Text*, Macmillan, London.

Haberler, G. (1958) *Prosperity and Depression*, 4th edn, Allen & Unwin, London.

Hahn, F. & Hollis, M. (1979) *Philosophy & Economic Theory*, Oxford University Press, Oxford.

Halsey, A.H. (1980) *Origins and Destinations: Family, Class and Education in Modern Britain*, Oxford University Press, Oxford.

Hannah, L. & Kay, J.A. (1977) *Concentration in Modern Industry*, Macmillan, London.

Haraszti, M. (1977) *A Worker in a Worker's State*, Penguin Books, Harmondsworth.

Harcourt, G.C. (1981) 'The Sraffian contribution: an evaluation', in Bradley & Howard (1981) *op. cit.*.

Harcourt, G.C. & Laing, N.F. (eds) (1971) *Capital and Growth*, Penguin Books, Harmondsworth.

Hargreaves Heap, S. (1980—81) 'World profitability crisis in the 1970s: some empirical evidence', *Capital and Class*, No. 12, Winter, pp. 66—84.

Harris, L. (1976) 'On interest, credit and capital', *Economy and Society*, Vol. V, No. 2, May, pp. 145—77.

Harrison, J. (1973) 'Productive & unproductive labour in Marx's political economy', *Conference of Socialist Economists Bulletin*, Vol. II.6, Autumn, pp. 70—82.

Harrison, J. (1978) *Marxist Economics for a Socialist: A Critique of Reformism*, Pluto Press, London.

Hicks, J.R. (1950) *A Contribution to the Trade Cycle*, Oxford University Press, Oxford.

Hicks, Sir John (1967) *Critical Essays in Monetary Theory*, Oxford University Press, Oxford.

Hilton, R. (ed.) (1976) *The Transition from Feudalism to Capitalism*, New Left Books, London.

Himmelweit, Susan & Mohun, S. (1975) 'The anomalies of capital', *Capital & Class*, No. 6, Autumn, pp. 67—105.

Hindess, B. & Hirst, P. (1977) *Mode of Production and Social Formation*, Macmillan, London.

Hobsbawm, G. (ed.) (1964) *Karl Marx: Precapitalist Economic Formations*. Lawrence & Wishart, London.

Hodgson, G. (1974) 'The theory of the falling rate of profit', *New Left Review*, No. 84, Mar.—April, pp. 55—82.

Hodgson, G. (1977) 'Papering over the cracks', in R. Miliband & J. Saville (eds), *Socialist Register*, Merlin Press, London.

Hollis, M. & Nell, E. (1975) *Rational Economic Man*, Cambridge University Press, Cambridge.
Horowitz, D. (ed.) (1968) *Marx and Modern Economics*, McGibbon & Kee, London.
Howard, M.C. & King, J.E. (1975) *The Political Economy of Marx*, Longman, Harlow.
Howard, M.C. & King, J.E. (eds) (1976) *The Economics of Marx*, Penguin Books, Harmondsworth.
Hunt, E.K. & Schwartz, J.G. (eds) (1972) *A Critique of Economic Theory*, Penguin Books, Harmondsworth.
Hussain, A. (1975) 'Marx's theory of money', mimeograph, University of Keele.
Itoh, M. (1975) 'The formation of Marx's theory of crisis'. *Conference of Socialist Economists Bulletin*, No. 10, February, pp. 1—19.
Itoh, M. (1976) 'A study of Marx's theory of value', *Science & Society*, Vol. 40, No. 3, Fall, pp. 307—40.
Itoh, M. (1980) *Value & Crisis: Essays on Marxian Economics in Japan*, Pluto Press, London.
Jones, Gareth Stedman (1972) 'Engels and the genesis of Marxism', *New Left Review*, No. 106, Nov.—Dec., pp. 79—104.
Jorgenson, D.W. (1967) 'The theory of investment behaviour', in R. Ferber (ed.), *Determinants of Investment Behaviour*, National Bureau of Economic Research (NBER), New York.
Junankar, P.N. (1972) *Investment: Theories and Evidence*, Macmillan, London.
Kalecki, M. (1943) 'Political aspects of full employment', *Political Quarterly*, Vol. 14. Reprinted in Hunt & Schwartz (1972) *op cit.*.
Kalecki, M. (1968) 'Trend and business cycle reconsidered', *Economic Journal*, Vol. LXXVIII, No. 310, pp. 263—76.
Kalecki, M. (1971) *Dynamics of the Capitalist Economy, 1933—1970*, Cambridge University Press, Cambridge.
Kay, G. (1975) *Development & Underdevelopment: A Marxist Analysis*, Macmillan, London.
King, M. (1975) 'The UK profits crisis: myth or reality?', *Economic Journal*, Vol. 85, No. 337, March, pp. 33—54.
King, J.E. (1979) 'Value & exploitation: some recent debates', *Discussion Paper* No. 4, April, University of Lancaster.
Kuhn, T.S. (1970) *The Structure of Scientific Revolutions*, 2nd edn, University of Chicago Press, Chicago.
Laclau, E. (1977) *Politics & Ideology in Marxist Theory*, New Left Books, London.
Laibman, D. (1977) 'Toward a Marxian model of growth', *American Economic Review*, Vol. 67, No. 1, Feb., pp. 387—92.
Latsis, S. (1976) *Method & Appraisal in Economics*, Cambridge University Press, Cambridge.
Lebowitz, M.A. (1976) 'Marx's falling rate of profit: a dialetical view', *Canadian Journal of Economics*, Vol. IX, No. 2, May, pp.232—54.

Levine, J. (1977) *Economic Studies: Contributions to the Critique of of Economic Theory*, Routledge & Kegan Paul, London.
McLellan, D. (ed.) (1977) *Karl Marx: Selected Writings*, Oxford University Press, Oxford.
Mandel, E. (1968) *Marxist Economic Theory*, Merlin Press, London.
Mandel, E. (1971) *The Formation of the Economic Thought of Karl Marx*, Monthly Review Press, New York.
Mandel, E. (1975) *Late Captialism*, New Left Books, London.
Marglin, S.A. (1976) *Value & Price in the Labour Surplus Economy*, Oxford University Press, Oxford.
Marris, R. (1964) *The Economic Theory of 'Managerial' Capitalism*, Macmillan, London.
Matthews, R.C.O. (1959) *The Trade Cycle*, James Nisbet & Co, Cambridge.
Mattick, P. (1969) *Marx & Keynes*, Merlin Press, London.
Medio, A. (1972) 'Profits and surplus value': appearance and reality in capitalist production', in Hunt & Schwartz *op.cit.*.
Meek, R.L. (1967) 'The falling rate of profit', in *Economics and Ideology and other Essays*, Chapman & Hall, London. Reprinted in Howard & King (1976) *op. cit.*
Meek, R.L. (1973) *Studies in the Labour Theory of Value*, 2nd edn, Lawrence & Wishart, London.
Meek, R.L. (1976) 'Whatever happened to the labour theory of value?', in M.J. Artis & A.R. Nobay (eds), *Essays in Economic Analysis*, Cambridge University Press, Cambridge.
Mészáros, I. (1975) *Marx's Theory of Alienation*, 4th edn, Merlin Press, London.
Morishima, M. (1973) *Marx's Economics*, Cambridge University Press, Cambridge.
Morishima, M. (1974a) 'Marx in the light of modern economic theory', *Econometrica*, Vol. 42, No. 4, July, pp. 611–32.
Morishima, M. (1974b) 'The fundamental Marxian theorem: a reply to Samuelson', *Journal of Economic Literature*, Vol. XII, No. 1, March, pp. 71–4.
Morishima, M. & Catephores, G. (1975) 'Is there an historical transformation problem', *Economic Journal*, Vol. 85, No. 338, June, pp. 309–28.
Morishima, M. & Catephores, G. (1978) *Value, Exploitation & Growth*, McGraw-Hill, London.
Morris, J. (1967) 'Marx as a monetary theorist', *Science & Society*, Vol. 31, No. 4, Fall, pp. 404–27.
Napoleoni, C. (1975) *Smith, Ricardo, Marx*, Basil Blackwell, Oxford.
Nell, E. (1973) 'Cyclical accumulation: a Marxian model of development', *American Economic Review*, Vol. LXIII, No. 2, May, pp.152–59.
Nordhaus, W. (1974) 'The falling share of profits', *Brookings Papers on Economic Activity*, No. 1, pp. 169–217.
Nove, A. & Nuti, D.M. (eds) (1972) *Socialist Economics*, Penguin Books, Harmondsworth.

Oakley, Allen (1977) 'A bibliographical analysis of Karl Marx's writings in political economy', *Research Report/Occasional Paper* No. 39, University of Newcastle, NSW Australia.

O'Connor, J. (1973) *The Fiscal Crisis of the State*, St. Martin's Press, New York.

Okishio, N. (1961) 'Technical change and the rate of profit', *Kobe University Economic Review*, Vol. 7, pp. 86–99.

Okishio, N. (1963) 'A mathematical note on Marxian theorems', *Weltwirtschaftliches Archiv*, Vol. 91, No. 2, pp. 287–98.

Ollman, Bertell (1976) *Alienation: Marx's Conception of Man in a Capitalist Society*, Cambridge University Press, Cambridge.

Pasinetti, L.L. (1977) *Lectures on the Theory of Production*, Columbia University Press, New York

Popper, K.R. (1966) *The Open Society and its Enemies*, Vol. 2, Routledge & Kegan Paul, London.

Radice, H. (ed.) (1975) *International Firms & Modern Imperialism*, Penguin Books, Harmondsworth.

Ricardo, D. (1951) *On the Principles of Political Economy and Taxation*, Vol. 1 of *The Works & Correspondence of David Racardo* (ed. P. Sraffa.) Cambridge University Press, Cambridge.

Rius (1976) *Marx for Beginners*, Writers & Readers' Cooperative, London.

Robinson, Joan (1966) *An Essay on Marxian Economics*, 2nd edn, Macmillan, London.

Roemer, J.E. (1977) 'Technical change and the "tendency of the rate of profit to fall"', *Journal of Economic Theory*, Vol. 16, Dec., pp. 403–24.

Roemer, J.E. (1978) 'The effect of technological change in the real wage and Marx's falling rate of profit', *Australian Economic Papers*, Vol. 17, No. 30, June, pp. 152–66.

Roemer, J.E. (1979) 'Continuing controversy on the falling rate of profit: fixed capital and other issues', *Cambridge Journal of Economics*, Vol. 3, No. 4, Dec., pp. 379–98.

Roemer, J.E. (1980) 'A general equilibrium approach to Marxian economics', *Econometrica*, Vol. 48, No. 2, March, pp. 505–30.

Rosdolsky, R. (1977) *The Making of Marx's 'Capital'*, Pluto Press, London.

Rowthorn, B. (1974a) 'Neo-classicism, neo-Ricardianism and Marxism', *New Left Review*, No. 86, July—Aug., pp. 63–87.

Rowthorn, B. (1974b) 'Skilled labour in the Marxist system', *Conference of Socialist Economists Bulletin*, Spring, pp. 25–45.

Rowthorn, B. (1980) *Capitalism, Conflict and Inflation*, Lawrence & Wishart, London.

Rubin, I.I. (1972) *Essays on Marx's Theory of Value*, Black & Red, Detroit.

Samuelson, P.A. (1957) 'Wages and interest: A modern dissection of Marxian economic models', *American Economic Review*, Vol. 47, No. 5, Dec., pp. 884–912.

Samuelson, P.A. (1962) 'Economists and the history of ideas', *American Economic Review*, Vol. 52, No. 1, March, pp. 1–18.

Samuelson, P.A. (1971) 'Understanding the Marxian notion of exploitation', *Journal of Economic Literature*, Vol. IX, No. 2, June, pp. 399–431.

Samuelson, P.A. (1974) 'Insight and detour in the theory of exploitation' and 'Rejoinder: Merlin unclothed; a final word', *Journal of Economic Literature*, Vol. XII, No. 1. March, pp. 75–7.

Schefold, B. (1976) 'Different forms of technical progress', *Economic Journal*, Vol. 86, No. 344, Dec., pp. 806–19.

Schumpeter, J.A. (1934) *The Theory of Economic Development*, Oxford University Press, New York. Reprinted 1963.

Schumpeter, J.A. (1954a), *Capitalism, Socialism and Democracy*, Allen & Unwin, London.

Schumpeter, J.A. (1954b) *History of Economic Analysis*, Allen & Unwin, London.

Schwartz, Jesse (ed.) (1977) *The Subtle Analysis of Capitalism*, Goodyear Publishing Co., Santa Monica.

Sen, A.K. (1977) 'Rational fools: A Critique of the behavioural foundations of economic theory', *Philosophy & Public Affairs*, Vol. 6, No. 4, pp. 317–44.

Sen, A.K. (1978) 'On the labour theory of value: some methodological issues' *Cambridge Journal of Economics*, Vol. 2, No. 2, June, pp. 175–90.

Seton, F. (1975) 'The transformation problem', *Review of Economic Studies*, Vol. XXIV(3), No. 65, June, pp. 149–60.

Shaikh, A. (1973) *Theories of Value and Theories of Distribution*, Ph. D. thesis, Columbia University.

Shaikh, A. (1977) 'Marx's theory of value and the "transformation problem"', in Schwartz *op. cit.*.

Shaikh, A. (1978) 'Political economy and capitalism: notes on Dobb's theory of crisis', *Cambridge Journal of Economics*, Vol. 2, No. 2, June, pp. 233–51.

Shaikh, A. (1980) 'The transformation from Sraffa to Marx (prelude to a critique of the neo-Ricardians)', mimeograph, March, New School for Social Research, New York.

Sherman, H.J. (1971) 'Marxist models of cyclical growth', *History of Political Economy*, Vol. 3, Spring, pp. 28–55.

Shoul, B. (1957) 'Karl Marx and Say's Law', *Quarterly Journal of Economy*, Vol. LXXI, Nov., pp. 611–29.

Sowell, T. (1960) 'Marx's "increasing misery" doctrine', *American Economic Review*, Vol. 50, No. 1, March, pp. 111–20.

Sowell, T. (1967) 'Marx's *Capital* after one hundred years', *Canadian Journal of Economics*, Vol. 33, pp. 50–74.

Sraffa, P. (1963) *Production of Commodities by Means of Commodities*, Cambridge University Press, Cambridge.

Steedman, I. (1977) *Marx after Sraffa*, New Left Books, London.

Steindl, J. (1952) *Maturity and Stagnation in American Capitalism*, Monthly Review Press, New York.

Sweezy, P. (1942) *Theory of Capitalist Development*, Monthly Review Press, New York.

Sweezy P.M. (1973a) 'Some problems in the theory of capital accumulation', *Bulletin of the Conference of Socialist Economists,* Autumn, pp. 25–36.

Sweezy, P.M. (ed.) (1973b) *Karl Marx and the Close of his System* by E. von Bohm Bawerk, A.M. Kelley, Clifton, New Jersey.

Sweezy, P.M. (1979) 'Marxian value theory & crises', *Monthly Review,* Vol. 31, No. 3, July–Aug., pp. 1–17.

Union for Radical Political Economics (1978) *US Capitalism in Crisis,* Union for Radical Political Economics, New York.

van Parijs, P. (1979) 'From contradiction to catastrophe', *New Left Review,* No. 115, May—June, pp. 87–96.

Walker, A. (1971) 'Karl Marx, the declining rate of profit and British political economy', *Economica,* Vol. 38, Nov., pp. 362–77.

Weisskopf, T.E. (1979) 'Marxian crisis theory and the rate of profit in the post-war US economy', *Cambridge Journal of Economics,* Vol. 3, No. 4, Dec., pp. 341–78.

Wilber, C.K. (ed.) (1973) *Political Economy of Development & Underdevelopment,* Random House, New York.

Winternitz, J. (1948) 'Values and prices: A solution to the so-called transformation problem', *Economic Journal,* Vol. 58, No. 230, June, pp. 276–80.

Wolff, B.D. (1978) 'Marxian crisis theory: structure & implications', *Review of Radical Political Economics,* Vol. 10. No. 1, Spring, pp.47–57.

Wolfstetter, E. (1973) 'Surplus labour, synchronised labour costs & Marx's labour theory of value', *Economic Journal,* Vol. 83, No. 331, Sept., pp. 787–809.

Wright, Erik Olin (1979) 'The value controversy & social research', *New Left Review,* No. 116, July—Aug., pp. 53–82.

Index